BREAK OPEN YOUR BOX

Piecing Your Life Together for a Time Such as This

Matthew M. Plank

Illustrated by Nicole Cowles

WESTBOW
PRESS®
A DIVISION OF THOMAS NELSON
& ZONDERVAN

Scripture quotations marked (NLT) are taken from the Holy Bible, New Living Translation, copyright © 1996, 2004, 2007 by Tyndale House Foundation. Used by permission of Tyndale House Publishers, Inc., Carol Stream, Illinois 60188. All rights reserved.

WestBow Press books may be ordered through booksellers or by contacting:

WestBow Press
A Division of Thomas Nelson & Zondervan
1663 Liberty Drive
Bloomington, IN 47403
www.westbowpress.com
1 (866) 928-1240

The Paradoxical Commandments are reprinted with the permission of the author. (c) Copyright Kent M. Keith 1968, renewed 2001, www.paradoxicalcommandments.com.

ISBN: 978-1-5127-9985-9 (sc)
ISBN: 978-1-5127-9986-6 (hc)
ISBN: 978-1-5127-9984-2 (e)

Library of Congress Control Number: 2017913153

Print information available on the last page.

WestBow Press rev. date: 09/29/2017

This book is dedicated to:

My personal Lord and Savior, Who died for my sins, so I could spend eternity with Him. Your Holy Spirit called me on this mission to inspire others. Thank you for trusting me and placing this assignment so heavily on my heart. I pray You continue to utilize me as Your instrument to spread the Good News.

My precious children, who have given me a new sense of passion and purpose. This book is meant to be your blueprint for building a meaningful life. I have great expectations for each of you. Always trust in God, and He will show you the way. I am so proud to be your dad, and I love you more than you will ever know.

My amazing family and friends, who have showered me with unconditional love and encouragement every step of the way. I will never be able to personally thank you enough for how deeply you have enriched my life. I sincerely hope these words speak to you and help you find your own God-given purpose.

Those yet to receive Christ, who are unaware of His everlasting mercy and grace. God is anxiously waiting to bless you beyond anything you can imagine. Seek Him, and watch your life transform before your very eyes. You will never make a more important decision. Take that leap of faith.

PREFACE

$\mathcal{I}$ remember quite vividly the day I decided to write this book. Having just returned from the doctor's office after hobbling on crutches for three weeks, I was attempting a nap on the couch, since sleep had eluded me the night before. I suppose I had been tormenting myself over what news was to come from the doctor. Already having endured one surgery in my life, I was hoping I wouldn't find myself lying on the operating table again.

So what led me to this moment on the couch? In February 2013, I set off with the guys on a skiing expedition to Colorado, looking for adventure. We certainly found it, although the medical ride that ensued wasn't quite what I had in mind. We intended to ski for three days, though I gracefully bowed out after day two (but I'm getting ahead of myself).

Day one was smooth sailing. The majority of the guys were advanced skiers, racing down the blue and black slopes. Thankfully, there was a rookie in our group who happened to be snapping his skis on for the first time. Let's just say the two of us weren't as effortless in our attempts down the mountain. We swallowed our pride and were perfectly content on the green paths. However, by the second day, our bravery arrived, and we mustered up the courage to tackle a few of the blue trails. Joining up with the rest of the crew, we gained confidence and officially became part of a well-oiled machine of skiers navigating the terrain.

While night skiing (which revealed a whole new perspective of absolutely breathtaking views) I decided to test my skills and conquer a trail I had been eyeing all day from the lift. Halfway down the Flying Dutchman, I felt invincible. Then, before I knew it, my right and left skis decided to go their separate ways, and I lost control. (In case you are wondering, communication is just as important for inanimate objects.) In that moment, I immediately realized this crash was different from those that had preceded. My right ski stayed on a wee bit too long, and when I hit the snow, I knew something wasn't right. After about five minutes testing my range of motion and convincing myself I could continue, I hesitantly finished my trek to the bottom. Long story not so short, I ended up fracturing a bone in my leg. During my first ski trip (four years prior), I managed to break my ski; on this outing, I broke my leg. In recapping these past experiences, I'm grasping the fact that the slopes haven't been so kind to me. Do I dare try a third time?

Nonetheless, this injury was the sole reason for my change of pace. I received the unique opportunity to relax, take some deep breaths, and evaluate my twenty-eight years of life. During those next four weeks, I was limited to one leg, and any walking required the assistance of my trusty crutches. Go figure, we also happened to be in the middle of one of the heaviest snowstorms our area had ever seen. Braving the outside world meant gingerly trudging around on a thick sheet of ice. Despite this challenge in the midst of frigid temperatures, my optimism prevailed, and I still somehow believed in those moments of restriction that I was the luckiest person in the world. I took my curiosity a step further and started thinking about the feelings that frequent my conscience from day to day. Even more importantly, I compared my state of mind to others. Let me ask you a question (and by the way, prepare yourself for many more to come): Have you ever wondered what is happening between the ears of others? I do—all the time.

I am often asked about my consistent state of happiness, and after receiving the same question time and time again, I finally asked myself, "Self, why do *I* get to be so happy?" Am I a rare breed? Definitely not. Do I possess secrets or insight others haven't successfully tapped into yet? Not likely. Have I been given the ability to help inspire others through my thoughts and ultimately my words? Maybe. In answering this last question, the ounce of possibility for a yes is what has led me here. I want to share with the world what I feel every single day in hopes that readers are able to fully enjoy life and all God has to offer. Even if this collection of thoughts only makes a difference for one soul, it will have served its intended purpose. I sincerely hope my message leaves a lasting imprint on your heart.

Forewarning: This will not be a book all about rainbows, fairies, and roses. I have faced suffering, adversity, and hardships, as all people have. What I have found from these first-hand experiences is they often provide the best times for personal growth. They challenge your character, show what you are made of, and put some hair on your chest, so to speak.

In my desire to put pen to paper, I am earnestly seeking to provoke your emotions and bring them to the surface. My focus is not geared toward a particular group of people; this is an open invitation. I welcome you to go on a journey with me. Are you an exhausted parent of five? An adolescent in search of guidance? Enchained to alcohol or another addiction? Newly diagnosed with cancer? On the brink of divorce? Contemplating suicide? Living in mediocrity and wanting more? Regardless of your previous road traveled and current situation, I pray there is a little something here for you and this message meets you right where you are today. Scripture-based examples will be highlighted at the end of each of the four parts. I encourage you to open the Bible, see the pages come to life, and find stories that are applicable to your own circumstances.

I want to interrupt your day-to-day routine. I want to awaken your senses and create a stirring inside your heart for more. I want to infuse purpose in your life and inspire you to achieve personal fulfillment. I challenge you to evaluate where you have been, where you are now, and where you want to go. Challenge accepted?

INTRODUCTION

$\mathcal{L}$ife is far more precious than we fully understand. It is the greatest gift we will ever receive. If we're being honest, life is also complex and intricate—a bit puzzle-esque. Think about it: The seconds, minutes, hours, days, months, years, and ultimately decades of our existence are a vast array of pieces. No one is like the other, as they all occupy their respective space.

When putting together a puzzle, I find it wise to implement a plan. The majority of puzzlers initially focus on constructing the border; this strategy allows the other pieces to better fall into place. Applying that same discipline in life helps us to build a solid, concrete framework of role models and influences, relationships, vocation, and faith. Then, through daily experiences, we fill in the empty gaps to complete our overall big picture.

We can certainly go rogue and ditch the idea of interlocking all edge pieces together. However, by substituting inner pieces to comprise the perimeter, we may find the finished product unrecognizable. I believe that just as jigsaw designers intend for their artwork to appear a particular way, God has a specific purpose for each and every one of us, a picture our lives are designed to create. And if our own individual puzzles are awry, how can we confidently bring a polished piece ready to integrate and proudly form the larger puzzle of mankind?

Herein lies the problem. Just as puzzle renegades may assume their vision of beauty is greater than the artist's, we have indicated our imagination is superior to God's divine plan. Funny, isn't it, how the majority of us don't live past eighty, while the Creator of the universe has been around since the beginning of time—yet we carry on as though we're the ones who know best. Even though we can't see the destination, we must trust in the journey. Once we agree to swallow our pride and work in communion with Him, we will finally begin to see our lives take shape. I believe that when we come to realize and fully appreciate His will for us, we will be awed by His mastery.

As you navigate these pages, my goal is for you to become aware of your own God-given pieces and to learn how and where to search for the missing ones. Know that I am praying for you in hope that you tear down your walls, invite Christ into your heart, and connect your pieces according to His will. I promise you that your dreams are nothing compared to what He has in store for you, and there will always be something missing without Him by your side.

Perspective is the key that unlocks true happiness. Each day you wake up, intentionally replace the questions of "What do I want for myself?" and "How can I make myself happy?" with "What does He want for me?" and "How can I make Him happy?" With that selfless and newly discovered conviction, break open your box for God. Let His creativity piece together the rest of your life. Offer up your time, talents, and treasures, and allow Him to use you as His instrument to enrich the lives of others.

Part 1

FIRST PUZZLE EDGE: ROLE MODELS AND INFLUENCES

Role Model: *A person who serves as a model in a particular behavioral or social role for another person to emulate.*
—The American Heritage College Dictionary

Remember your leaders who taught you the word of God. Think of all the good that has come from their lives, and follow the example of their faith.
—Hebrews 13:7

Chapter 1

PARENTING:
FROM A CHILD'S PERSPECTIVE

$\mathcal{W}$ith our puzzle analogy still fresh in mind, let's get to work and start assembling your four edges: role models and influences, relationships, vocation, and faith. When it comes to leaving a legacy for others to stand on, one building block carries the most weight— the apotheosis, if you will: faith. You can bet your bottom dollar this will later be addressed, but for now, let's delve into the rest of the mix. There's no better place to start than with role models and influences, the most natural of which are parents.

Do we need parents? Some kids would say no. I mean, surely (who's Shirley?), we can figure everything out on our own accord, right? This was my adopted viewpoint as a youngster. Having since gained a little wisdom (and a few wrinkles), I laugh and wholeheartedly disagree with my teenage self. And hopefully by the time we've laid down our first edge of the puzzle, I will have made a strong case for the invaluable life lessons parents and role models instill in subsequent generations.

Understanding Our Challenge

We were all brought into this world as blank slates; we knew nothing about everything. Our selfishness commenced right out of the chute.

We cried and continued to do so until we got what we wanted, whether sleep, food, comfort, or a clean diaper. Our only concern was what we needed and what would make us happy. There was no regard for others, because we didn't know any better; we were ignorant. (For clarification, "ignorant" doesn't mean stupid, but rather lacking in knowledge.)

Many would agree that crying is a communication method newborns use to meet their most basic needs. And at the age of two, snatching a toy or yanking someone's hair is not uncommon. The terms "right" and "wrong" don't hold any value to us in our early years. Self-indulgence, recklessness, and disrespect at a young age don't pose an immediate threat to society. But when does that self-centered behavior become a detriment to others? Because selfishness is innate, selflessness must be modeled and learned. If it is not, and there is no intervention from a parental figure, these negative manners will often continue in adolescence and on into adulthood. What's worse is that they are often passed on to future offspring, creating an endless cycle of family dysfunction.

Hypothetically speaking, a young, naïve teenager who breaks into an elderly woman's house may not fully comprehend the significance of his actions. He is apathetic about the personal possessions he steals, including a diamond necklace (that has been a family heirloom for two hundred years) and cash on the nightstand, meant to spoil the woman's great-granddaughter on her first birthday. The juvenile's primary concern is the task at hand: earning the respect of his newfound friends.

Who am I to blame him for seeking approval and wanting to feel a sense of belonging? Don't we all yearn for that? Traditionally, parental figures lovingly supply an endless amount of acceptance without a second thought. (Although at a disadvantage, those without involved parents aren't lost by any means, as we will see.) Without a sense of security at home and guidance on how to build healthy relationships, kids are emotionally deprived and often left casting their desperate pleas of acceptance onto an unworthy crowd. At this crucial age of character development, they are ill-informed yet able to learn.

My Testimonial

In my own reflection, I appreciate more and more how fortunate I was to have phenomenal mentors along the way. As each day passes, I thank my heavenly Father for all the blessings He has bestowed upon me, two of which are an incredible mom and dad. Let's meet them.

"Selfless" is my mother Julie's middle name. (Okay, fine, it's actually Kathleen.) She successfully passed that invaluable trait to one of her children. (And no, that's not me.) In fact, I'm not even sure she understands what it means to receive, unless what she's receiving is the blessing of endless giving.

Outside of church, her sanctuary is the kitchen. In another life, she would be one of the world's best bakers. She still is; the rest of the world just doesn't know it yet. When someone loses a family member, my mom delivers a home-cooked meal. On a birthday or special occasion, a batch of her famous chocolate chip cookies or a favorite dessert is right around the corner. She understands that the way to a person's heart is often through the stomach, and she fills it plumb full.

She harbors a true mother's instinct, has always provided for me throughout my life, and certainly still does to this day. When I throw her the look that says, "Mom, I got this," she lovingly exclaims, "I'm sorry, but I can never stop being a mom." What I value the most in being her son is learning firsthand how to be genuine, compassionate, and truly caring toward others. She tells me hugs are candy for the soul, and I now love handing them out like it's Halloween night.

My father, Michael, is a friend of the world. As a child, I remember thinking that no matter where we went, he always seemed to know someone. Others gravitated toward him. His energy and zest for life have led my wife to endearingly describe him as "a lunatic—in the best way possible."

My pa is a simple man at heart, whose entertainment could be watching a fire burn all night. He introduced me to the sport of people-watching, which quickly became one of our favorite pastimes. When the girls (my mom and sisters) would take us shopping, my dad thoroughly enjoyed connecting with anyone and everyone, and still does. He will have you exchanging life stories only minutes after meeting. (You can blame him for the mass quantity of questions in this book.) He and I aren't likely to limit our conversations to just talking about the weather; we would rather delve into where your passions lie, why you make the decisions you do, and what makes your heart full. He has ultimately shown me how to be a good father, and for that, I can't ever thank him enough. The intensity of love he unwaveringly expresses for his family is incredible.

Together, my mom and dad have demonstrated what a loving relationship looks like. As I reflect on my childhood, sure, my sisters and I observed their quarreling now and then, but most disputes were handled privately. In recalling the first time I ever heard a voice raised, I immediately thought the worst and desperately inquired, "Are you guys getting a divorce?" After witnessing my parents' love and commitment over the past thirty-two years, I can comfortably affirm that separation was never an option. They are now relishing their new phase of life and love as grandparents. (They seem to excel at that too.)

If Abraham Maslow (creator of the hierarchy of human needs) had ever made an unannounced visit to the Plank household during my upbringing, he would have acknowledged that all my physiological needs were met and exceeded on a daily basis. I was alive and breathing, there was always plenty of food on the table, and water was in abundance. Progressing beyond the fundamental level, it would have been easy for him to see that I constantly felt safe and loved, and I was encouraged to pursue my dreams.

That's not to say that when I was under my parents' roof, I fully agreed with (or even comprehended) all of the discipline I felt was strictly enforced. However, I wasn't given much of a choice, and I reluctantly followed their rules. I laugh now about the dreaded and often-used line, "You'll understand when you are older." Sure enough, Mom and Dad, I must be older, because those teaching moments are beginning to make sense. Had their words of wisdom not been preached in my ear during the introductory years, I might very well have been the silhouette raiding the aforementioned elderly woman's home.

Leaving the Nest

Obviously, your parents can't physically hold your hand every second; let's be honest, you probably wouldn't want them to either. Many of you are living on your own, and independence has already long been established. For those who aren't, there will come a time to leave the nest. You will hold your breath, spread your wings, and hope to soar. At that point, your parents will likely clasp their hands, close their eyes, and pray their guidance was enough. The true test will present itself when you look around and your parents are nowhere to be seen; suddenly, it's just you in this big world. Are you prepared?

Life will throw you countless twists and turns; in fact, you will go through a drastic range of emotions, not only from day to day, but even from hour to hour. It's important that you remember the lifelong lessons your parents (or parental figures) ingrained in you. Be true to yourself; maintain your identity and integrity, no matter how difficult the situation. Your character defines who you are. Your personality should always control your emotions, not the other way around. You must stay grounded in times of success and triumph yet not fall flat during bouts of misfortune or failure.

Personal Example: Valley

After redshirting my first year on the college basketball team and then only enjoying mercy minutes on the court during the second season, my head coach sat me down and delivered "the talk." In his evaluation, I didn't possess the necessary skills to perform at the collegiate level. (To this day, I still disagree.) I won't lie; that kind of rejection was a heavy blow. My pride and reputation as an athlete were tarnished in my eyes, but what seemed like a tough pill to swallow was only a small hiccup in reality. Bear with me as we take an extreme hypothetical journey of how this scenario could have played out without a solid head on my shoulders. Take note of how fast our lives can spin out of control from even the tiniest setback.

I *could* have completely lost my self-esteem, which *could* have carried over into other aspects of my life. Feeling defeated, I *could* have lacked the necessary motivation for my academics. In turn, my grades *could* have suffered, and my initial thought of playing hooky *could* have turned into a weekly game. This free time *could* have opened up a whole new social network, with numerous temptations at my fingertips. One of those enticing invitations *could* have been trying drugs for the first time. Suddenly, my lackadaisical attitude *could* have led to me skipping the majority of my fall semester, dropping out of college, forfeiting my professional aspirations, dealing drugs to earn extra cash, and ultimately ending up behind bars.

If I wasn't careful, all of those "could" statements might have very well turned into real-life regrets. One of the most common phrases you hear coming from the losing team after hard-fought competition, and one I have to admit I have muttered before, is, "We should have won that game." Coulda, shoulda, woulda, but didn't. However, in this case, we are talking about something far more important than a loss on the court or field, but rather a setup for failure in the game of life. In that exaggerated series of events, I *coulda* put more focus on my degree, I *shoulda* made the D.A.R.E. officer proud and said no to drugs, and I *woulda* had a better chance of graduating with honors and landing my dream job.

Personal Example: Peak

On the contrary, this next example is one of accomplishment. After nervously and frantically fumbling with the envelope, I learned of my acceptance into the University of Kansas School of Pharmacy (Rock Chalk, Jayhawk, KU). Let's follow another theoretical tangent, one in which my viewpoints are obviously egotistically skewed. That feat definitely brought congratulatory celebration from those near and far, but I *could* have gotten carried away and let the excitement consume me. This overabundance of confidence *could* have unknowingly led to arrogance and *could* have caused me to forget about my true friends. My mentality *could* have been that I was moving into the city, on to bigger and better things, and leaving my past in the dust. I likely wouldn't have even noticed a tripwire on the ground with my head held as such. However, the intense curriculum *could* have proven too difficult midway through the program, forcing me to quit and shattering my professional dreams. I *could* have returned home with my tail between my legs to the assumed comfort and support of my childhood friends. Instead, I *could* have been met with the door I closed on those relationships when my ego ballooned. As a result, I *could* have been left living under a mountain of student loans, wallowing in my own self-pity.

While I admit these cascading effects are unlikely, they might hit a little closer to home than we would care to acknowledge. What memories of past setbacks and excitement come to mind for you? How did they play out? Why? Timely discipline and unconditional love from our parents afford us the ability to keep our composure during the highs and lows life will inevitably throw our way. The eloquent balance of these two factors is critical as we construct our puzzle border.

Chapter 2

PARENTING: FROM A PARENT'S PERSPECTIVE

My Testimonial

There is no greater opportunity to be a role model and influence others than when God bestows on you a beautiful baby. I have previously discussed one side of the coin. Now a dad of two under two, I would like to share my fresh perspective on the flip side.

I will never forget the day my wife, Holly, told me I was going to be a dad. I was in the bathroom combing my hair. Allow me the latitude to digress for a second. I don't normally use a comb; I didn't even own a comb the previous month. I usually get out of the shower, quickly run my hands through my hair, occasionally style with gel, and call it good. However, we had recently returned from a once-in-a-lifetime European vacation. Prior to departing, I went for a quick trim. Everything in me wanted to tell my barber to keep it looking professional, like I normally do. Yet, this particular day, I was feeling anything but normal.

I said, "I'm getting ready to leave for Europe, I'm feeling brave, and I wanna look like a local." Voila—out I came with a pompadour, hair glue, and my first comb.

Fast-forward four weeks, and my hair still screamed I was overseas, baguette in hand. We have since parted ways (pun intended). So there I was, combing my hair in front of the mirror, when out of my peripheral vision, I saw Holly sneak into the room. Before I knew it, I was glancing down at two pink lines on a stick my grinning wife anxiously displayed. Thanks to country singer Eric Church, I knew what said lines indicated. Apparently, I repeatedly asked, "Are you serious?" while simultaneously backing up inch by inch. I continued to tiptoe further away in disbelief until I was at the back of our closet, with nowhere to go. Shortly after, the flood gates opened, and out came the water works. We were thinking, laughing, and crying all in a matter of seconds. The late Jimmy Valvano would have been proud of that morning. (If that sentence didn't register, Google Valvano's ESPY speech. You will be glad you did.) Then Holly and I shared a warm embrace and thanked God for the start of what was sure to be an incredible journey.

I remember the anticipation building day-by-day for the culmination of the pregnancy and the moment we could peer into those precious little eyes. Learning so much about the human body and God's creative wonders kept us enthralled throughout the progression of those 38.5 weeks. We were in awe at the first sonogram, as well as every subsequent viewing. All the tiny body parts, from her spine and ribs to her fingers and toes, were so intricately and perfectly formed in a few short months. Learning about our baby's development each week and seeing her on the big screen were definitely highlights. Future dads, FYI, your involvement is not only welcomed during the exciting benchmark visits, but also much appreciated and expected in the everyday quirks of the incubation period.

In my experience as a first-time father, with no doubt still much to learn, I fully recognize there are certain unspoken obligations during your wife's pregnancy. You have no right to complain about requests to drive across town late at night to satisfy cravings. Maybe, by happenstance, the whole bag of juicy peaches from the local grocery store your wife savagely consumed will be recalled, with the possibility of listeria contamination. You should happily oblige by digging to the bottom of the previous day's trash and investigating the evidence of any peach remains. Yes, I speak from firsthand experience and am thrilled to report a "Big Smile" sticker indicated we were in the clear (whew ...).

You may have to resort to bestowing your lady with kisses like European royalty, cheek-to-cheek, whenever your breath is too pungent and runs the risk of intensifying her nausea. Our guilty culprits were eggs, onions, bananas, and other odorous cuisine; unscented Febreze was our friend. Your housework requirements and honey-do lists may drastically increase, because your wife is exhausted on the couch, counter, dryer, stairs, or wherever she happens to rest her pretty little head. Holly couldn't help but sneak a nap in random places throughout our home, and yes, I have digital evidence.

I specifically remember her words: "Honey, I'm sorry I'm so worthless."

I replied, "Sweetheart, you are worth more now than ever. You are growing our baby girl. I will take care of everything else." It was true.

Through various literature and word of mouth, we learned babies can hear muffled tones from the outside world. I was strongly encouraged to talk to our baby in the womb so she could begin to recognize my voice. Gentlemen, listen up: There are a handful of life-changing moments containing the power to stop time. This was one of them for me. Because I heeded the advice of our doctor and friends, I will always cherish the following memory. Immediately after our daughter Paisley was born, a nurse laid her on my wife's chest, as skin-to-skin contact is beneficial for early bonding. When Paisley was being handed up to Holly, I said softly, "Hi Paisley, it's Daddy," to my little girl for our first conversation outside the womb. My daughter instantly turned her beautiful blue eyes and locked onto mine.

Prior to that day, I distinctly remember watching the faces of rookie dads when I badgered one after another about that first interaction with their newborn. Their look said it all, and I quickly came to understand why. I pray God has mine on tape; that fleeting moment was as close to heaven on earth as I have ever experienced.

Deep in prayer earlier that morning, I pleaded for God to make me a channel of His peace and allow me to simply be present in the delivery room to provide support. I'm naturally a squeamish person around blood and guts, so believe me when I say I was prepared for the worst and had no intention of watching. Not only did I overcome my fear of passivity, but I recall two separate accounts in the journal I kept involving Holly scolding my surprisingly energetic demeanor. While in the valley between contractions, she said, "Honey, I love you, but shut up," and "Go away; stop looking at me." Oops. The calm that came over me was seriously astonishing. Jesus quieted the sea of my nerves, as He did for His disciples in Mark 4:39. I was mesmerized while I watched everything and even managed to be a little hands-on. With a clear mind, my emotions were free to be in full swing throughout the wee hours of that Saturday morning. Sustained happiness, endless thankfulness, pure bliss, nonstop excitement, much uncertainty, paralyzing fear, growing curiosity, driving adrenaline; they all coexisted.

Paisley had us wrapped around her little half-inch finger from the moment we laid eyes on her; we didn't stand a chance. I couldn't get over the fact that she was my baby girl, and I was her daddy. I would be remiss if I didn't boast about my amazing wife's mental strength in that delivery room. She endured bouts of intense pain without a trace of medication; she was a rock star, and I was beyond proud. When a minute to catch our breath arrived, we gazed at each other in disbelief. We were officially parents, a family of three (and now four), and this was our new life. God blessed us with a miracle—an absolute miracle—not only once, but now twice.

First-Time Parent?

Despite minimal years (admittedly) on the high parental seas, I am still anxious to share my newfound wisdom. Teamwork makes the dream work; rely on each other. Join together as a united front, and remember: You are the parent first, and their friend second. While you may seem unpopular and disliked from time to time, your kids will one day understand that discipline is a necessary form of parental love.

There are plenty of parenting resources available, but none of them are guaranteed to work on *your* child. Each child is unique, and sometimes (most times), you simply learn as you go. You will experience waves of emotions throughout your life with a little one. Some days, you may be on the upper deck of a cruise ship basking in the sun, as you effortlessly glide across the calm surface of smiles, coos, and cuddles. Other days, you could find yourself at the bottom of a rundown vessel, hanging on for dear life, while you brave a chaotic storm of diapers, spit-up, and incessant wailing. Whenever your ship sets sail on those uncharted waters, I hope to have steered you in the right direction.

Please don't take your position at the helm for granted, because there are couples who want nothing more than to have their own children. Treat parenting like a privilege, not a right. Accept that privilege and know how much responsibility is attached, starting from day one, or as my wife has since corrected me, from conception. (She's right.) You will likely be offered help, and you will need it. In the words of a dear late friend, "Give graciously, but also learn to receive graciously." Trust me: It's a win for both parties. Accepting help is not showing weakness, and you are not a burden to others. Rejecting their offer is denying them of the blessing to serve. And remember: Making others happy is how one finds their own true happiness.

Here's a very important lesson for all working parents: Don't be the one who spends too much time at the office, missing all the firsts your child will inevitably have. Limit the occasions you sacrifice dance recitals, science fairs, and sporting events for travel, meetings, and late nights on the job. Allow your face to be visible when your little ones eagerly scan the crowd. Half of the task is simply showing up. In the wise words of an experienced father, "Sweat is cheap." When you are home with impressionable minds nearby, avoid being immersed in the television or phone. Don't let electronics have priority over being an active father or mother. Be all in, and give your kids undivided attention. Make it a point to devote quality time and develop a special bond early. "I wish I would have spent more time working," said no one on their death bed ever. Realize what is most important, and show your family you understand their needs.

Recognize Your Significance as a Parent

Who do your kids come home to every night? I have read the statistics, and the numbers are staggering. Children with a mother and father in the same home who demonstrate a loving, healthy marriage, are provided with an essential foundation. Of course, there are amazing stories of exceptions to this statement. Many single moms and dads are the epitome of determination and hard work, thus instilling discipline and respect in their offspring. Yet my introductory question remains to parents who are not actively present: "Why not you?" Even if tears aren't visible on the outside, your child may be desperately crying for your attention on the inside. If you currently have innocent, little eyes looking up to you for direction, ask yourself if you would be making Maslow proud, and hold your children extra tight tonight, knowing what a precious gift from God they are.

Rewind the biological clock and think back to your younger years, when you saw the world through those innocent eyes. Were your parents around for the big occasions? What about the day-to-day activities? Did you feel safe and protected? Did your parents keep their promises? Did they set good examples for you to follow? My responses to those questions all checked out to be yes. How about yours? All in all, do you feel your parents were positive influences on you?

Another way to affirmatively answer that final question is to let your everyday behavior be a testament. One day, while casually conversing with an older gentleman, he inquired about my parents. Of course I told him God blessed me with some of the best. He proceeded to attest that my upbringing was apparent through my consideration for others. That's it, folks. Let your character shine through your actions, not only giving your kids someone to emulate, but also making your parents proud. That friendly stranger gave me one of the most meaningful compliments I have received to date. I called my mom and dad later that night, because the gentleman's praise was a direct tribute to their cumulative thirty-two years of parenting. I cringe, imagining my life without their guiding hands every step of the way. No, I don't pretend to hold all the answers—not even close, but I had two pretty special people to lay the foundation. With their passing of the torch, the *onus* is now *on us* to follow the blueprint and keep the flame alive for our children.

Chapter 3

INFLUENCES
OUTSIDE THE HOME

Looking for a Mentor?

*O*utside of home life, we need to be careful where our admiration shines, especially with high-profile artists, athletes, and actors. On the surface, some celebrities appear to have it all: mansions, fancy sports cars, arm candy, and more money than you can possibly fathom. They may portray the perfect life, but the exposed glamour might not match up with what is truly happening behind the curtain. Hollywood stars take their turn shining bright but can be quick to flicker and eventually burn out. In their prime, they have the world at their fingertips and rarely hear the word no. They often appear invincible and push the limits of life, which can lead to irreversible damage. Scandalous affairs, law-breaking behavior, and disguised emotional distress can all spell disaster in their respective ways. We can find countless examples of each on the front of tabloids with regularity, as their lives are constantly viewed under a microscope. (We common folk have the same problems; our dirty laundry just isn't nationally aired.)

Usually, a tarnished reputation is the biggest consequence. In extreme cases, lives are lost. I think back to one of the most vocally gifted musicians. She could have sung the phone book, and I would have intently listened. Sadly, she succumbed to drug abuse, leaving this world far too early from an overdose. Most recently was the tragedy surrounding a comedian who held humor in spades. This man always captivated his audience and most certainly knew how to fill a room. I used to get bellyaches watching his impromptu ingenuity on prime time. I'm sure I echo the majority of America in saying how oblivious I was to the degree he masked his suffering. It was heartbreaking to learn of his underlying emptiness, as his long-standing depression led him to suicide. Whitney and Robin, you are missed; God rest your souls.

I know these isolated examples don't speak for all of Hollywood, and not every celebrity goes down a treacherous path. Some amazing role models stand out from the crowd, and what a platform they have to reach the masses. (Keep preaching the word, Steph Curry, Drew Brees, Carrie Underwood, Chris Pratt, and all who adamantly represent.) I include this section to reach the community who stares in amazement and may be drowning in a sea of jealousy, not to bash Hollywood. Sure, celebs bask in the limelight, but I bet you would be hard-pressed to find one who hasn't been envious of you (yeah, you) a time or two. You may disagree, but hear me out. Whenever they venture out of their estate, hiding is no easy feat. After signing umpteen autographs, there may be a hint of disappointment in their eyes. You see, on that particular evening, their goal upon leaving the house might have been to relax, dine uninterrupted, and enjoy some quality family time. Perhaps this obscurity sounds like the norm for you and yours, something you often take for granted. For them, it's nearly impossible to come by. My message is simply this: Our lives and theirs are worlds apart, so we shouldn't make comparisons. Fame and riches are temporary, but honesty and righteousness stand the test of time. The lesson here is that we should appreciate our lives and not wish to live another's. In the words of Oscar Wilde, "Be yourself; everyone else is already taken."

If you still haven't found good role model material, you may be losing hope. Fear not, because your lights aren't turned out yet. Never give yourself an excuse to fail or let your past prevent you from making something of yourself. Seek out those you aspire to emulate for guidance on how to break open your own box and set your border. My best advice is to identify someone who can provide you with the direction and encouragement you need. Perhaps a grandparent or other family member is your solution. If not, explore beyond your gene pool and assess the people around you. Who exemplifies characteristics worth following? My initial suggestions would be a friend, pastor, teacher, counselor, coach, church member, coworker, or a friend's parent. Are there any names that come to mind? Mentally or physically, jot down the reasons why. How do they carry themselves? Do they have a genuine nature to their character? Do they treat others with kindness? How do they handle stress? Do they understand you and offer a calming presence? After carefully narrowing down your search, all that's left is to ask someone into your life. No matter the surrounding influences you follow, be sure you always recognize the person staring back at you in the mirror.

Hoping to Be a Mentor?

Now, exchanging roles in this situation, let's imagine you were recently asked to offer your wisdom and guidance. The amount of responsibility implied might initially draw hesitation, but your first reaction should be one of honor. Smile knowing you were chosen; what a compliment to the way you live your life. This is an exciting challenge you've been handed, as you now have added accountability of your daily behaviors. In all likelihood, you won't have to make drastic changes to your lifestyle. Your current actions are positively catching someone's attention, so keep calm and role model on. With your newfound audience, keep striving to reach even higher standards. Every future action you perform and word you speak carries more weight than ever. In a world of endless talkers, be the doer who doesn't need to say anything to be heard. As St. Francis of Assisi shared, "Preach the Gospel at all times, and when necessary, use words."

Going through the Motions?

How about the rest of you? I initially shared that my hope in writing this book was to reach all walks of life. Maybe there hasn't been something for you to write home about quite yet. Be patient; we are just getting started, and these next few pages might be the ones to pique your interest. If you are a lost soul searching for your purpose, let's infuse some meaning into your life. You're probably aware there are a vast number of children and adolescents (and quite frankly, some adults) who need direction. In all likelihood, you won't literally receive a tap on your shoulder asking for help. The great news is this mentoring role certainly isn't limited to specific professions or relationships. Why not step up to the plate and swing for the fences? Forget reactive; be proactive. Throughout your daily conversations and interactions, carefully observe others. What are they most in need of? See the world like never before. Listen to Matthew West's song, "My Own Little World," and learn from it. Pray your eyes are opened and watch all the opportunities unfold.

For those with a Y chromosome, the book *The Resolution for Men* by Stephen & Alex Kendrick and Randy Alcorn is a great reference to initiate a spark in becoming the man you want to be. If you are in agreement on setting the right tone, but aren't sure where to begin, I suggest you start with the following essential elements we should be pouring into undeveloped minds:

- When greeting someone, offer a solid, firm handshake and make eye contact to show you are fully engaged. Sincerely acknowledge all people in your daily travels. If you ask a question ("Hi, how are you?"), be sure to stick around long enough to listen to the answer. Otherwise, limit your encounter to a friendly greeting and smile as you pass by.
- Treat women with respect. Prove chivalry is not dead; be a gentleman. Regularly open doors and pull out chairs. Buy "just because" flowers and write thoughtful notes.

Stay spontaneous and surprise loved ones with meaningful expressions.

• Turn off electronics in the midst of company. Converse with those around you when dining with colleagues, classmates, friends, or loved ones. Be all in and make them feel important. No form of technology demands your attention like the faces in front of you. I firmly believe this little pearl can be a means to keeping your family close, no matter how hectic your lives may become.

Obviously, this is an abbreviated list, but it can hopefully offer fertile ground for your mentoring roots to grow. A living example is illustrated by the verses of "Watching You" by Rodney Atkins. Be aware of your actions, and don't let prime teaching moments slip away. You never know when someone might be peeking around the corner, ready to imitate your every move. Oftentimes, the actions or gestures we consider small or insignificant prove to be monumental for those eager to learn.

For those who feel they can't fulfill an advisory position to a youngster, wouldn't this be a great opportunity to reassess your situation? Do you want to make something of yourself? Don't blindly continue the route your ancestors started you down. You are not required to pass a destructive torch on to the next generation. It only takes one person, *you*, to change the status quo and break the chain of self-destruction. And that change can start today.

Chapter 4

FROM THE LIVING WORD: DANIEL'S EXTRAORDINARY INFLUENCE

What is the Bible, other than the best-selling piece of literature of all time? The Bible is a God-inspired compilation of sixty-six books written by over forty different authors (ranging from shepherds to doctors) that spans about sixteen centuries. The writings, which consist of laws, narratives, poetry, parables, testimonies, and more, are broken up into two main parts: the Old and New Testaments.

The Old Testament tells the story of creation, reveals God's original intention for humanity, and shows us the sin that brought evil into the world. The writings narrate the early church, with a magnifying glass over the rise and fall of God's chosen people, the Israelites. Prophecies are hidden throughout the chapters, foreshadowing a master plan of redemption.

The New Testament fulfills all the prophecies of the Old Testament and ultimately introduces us to our redeemer, Jesus Christ. He is God, in human form, Who came to live among us as *the* ultimate example. The text follows His thirty-three years of life on earth. Through their teachings, Jesus' disciples, His right-hand men, proclaim that although He was brutally killed, He overcame death and was resurrected into heaven, leading the way for all of us to be saved and live for eternity. Throughout the remainder of the New Testament, the disciples spread His story and love to all. The Bible ends with the promise of His return for judgment to declare our eternal destinations. (Believe me, I've never understood the reasoning behind our salvation, but I certainly have the utmost appreciation.)

Seek the red ink (which indicates the words from the mouth of Jesus) in the Bible, and you will find yourself in the midst of some of the most unforgettable moments in history. Jesus was, is, and will always be the best role model and influence Who has ever walked this earth. During a spiritual retreat I attended one fall, the priest gave a very moving introduction to the weekend. He challenged us all individually to deny our self, pick up our daily cross, and follow Christ. I thank him for that unequivocal reminder of Whose footsteps we should walk in. I know how the saying normally goes, but be that as it may, you would be wise to put all your eggs in Jesus' basket.

Those red-lettered words of God's divine Son could be the prime examples in all of these remaining chapters. However, let's broaden our biblical horizons as we explore outside His crimson words. I discovered a plethora of remarkable mentors while digging through scripture. One of the first who jumped off the pages was Daniel, the star of a twelve-chapter book near the end of the Old Testament. While chapters 7 through 12 elaborate on his visions, which are extraordinary in their own right, I want to draw your attention to the first six chapters. There is a tremendous amount to gain from studying this heroic man. One of the most important teaching points I want to drive home is that Daniel yearned for guidance from the Lord. He prayed three times a day, every day. I can't tell you how often I fall short of this discipline. The sentiment, "God doesn't talk to me," is something I hear frequently. Are we setting aside the necessary time to listen? Contrary to popular practice, praying isn't comprised of kneeling, folding your hands, bowing your head, and asking for God's help in a monologue. Equally important is to open your ears, mind, heart, and soul to receive His message. If you desire a deeper relationship with your almighty Father, daily *dialogue* in prayer is essential.

Through Daniel's routine worship, he developed a connection to God we should all strive for. Daniel lived during an era of one of the most vicious blows dealt by the hand of God. Because of the sinful nature of His people, God directed the Babylonians to completely destroy Jerusalem. Daniel, along with the other Israelites, was taken into captivity and led to Babylon. Although the rationale was not conveyed to Daniel, he trusted the Lord and continued to pray, giving praise to God through the storm. What can we learn from this obedience? We don't always have to know the plan, as long as we place our trust in the One Who does. As we continue to read, hardships were ever-present, along with countless temptations, but Daniel never lost his faith.

When he arrived in Babylon, Daniel stood out among all the other Israelites to King Nebuchadnezzar. As a result, he was hand-selected to serve in the king's palace, receiving a three-year education on the language and literature of the Babylonian culture. Along with this royal treatment was a right to the delectable choice meat and wine from the king's table. Daniel knew the decision to partake would defile his body and the temple it was, as the laws of the Old Testament forbid certain foods. He pleaded with the officials, who allowed his (and his friends') diet to consist of vegetables and water alone, with the agreement that their strength and physique would be evaluated and compared with the others eating the assigned meals. By God's grace, they appeared healthier and better nourished than those dining in elegance. Admittedly, this self-control from edible temptation was far surpassed by the bravery he later showed, but it proved a very meaningful point to God nonetheless. Daniel passed the test, albeit small, and therefore was graciously protected under God's almighty wing. Applying this to our own lives, how can we expect our Creator to bestow extraordinary measures upon us when we can't be entrusted with the ordinary?

Daniel was a phenomenal leader who earned the respect of those around him, which included a great supporting cast of three close friends—Shadrach, Meshach, and Abednego. Their faith in God was iron strong when put on trial, as they were ordered to assimilate with a crowd of thousands, bowing down to a golden statue of the Babylonian king. Honoring the First Commandment, they unwaveringly refused to worship another god and fully accepted death as their punishment. All three men were afforded a second chance to surrender, but each remained steadfast. As a consequence, they were bound and thrown into a blazing furnace by the king's soldiers. Because of their proximity to the roaring flames, the escorting soldiers instantly burned to death. As for Shadrach, Meshach, and Abednego, they were under the care of a heavenly bodyguard. To the king's amazement, all three fearless men walked out unbound and unharmed, without a single hair singed on their heads. The degree of resolve you can muster when being led by a man of Daniel's caliber is truly astounding.

Another inspiring testimony to his faith, through which Daniel received his claim to fame, occurred in the lions' den. Because Daniel was a man of high regard, his colleagues were envious of the special treatment awarded to him by the new king, Darius the Mede. I once heard the phrase, "You aren't someone in the world until you have a few critics." Daniel definitely endured his fair share of opposition. As it would happen, other administrators within the royal court persuaded the king to enforce a new law. The law, intended to target Daniel and his homage to his personal Lord, stated that those who prayed to anyone other than King Darius would be tossed into the lions' den. Despite this terrifying death sentence, Daniel steadfastly continued to pray to God three times a day, his windows open for all to observe. He was inevitably sentenced to the den, but his life was spared when the lions' mouths were miraculously closed. Daniel's accusers were then locked in the same den and torn to shreds before they hit the ground. The moral of the story: God protects His loyal and faithful servants.

We can also learn from those in the book of Daniel who were sinful with pride. During the time of Daniel, King Nebuchadnezzar became arrogant, consequently lost his kingdom, and resorted to actually grazing with cattle. Upon being humbled and acknowledging his power was a result of the glory of God rather

---

From the Living Word: Daniel's Extraordinary Influence

than his own doing, he was restored to his authoritative position. However, his successor, Belshazzar, didn't prove to be as wise. He blatantly praised other gods and continued his disrespect by enjoying wine out of God's gold and silver cups that had previously been stolen from the temple. You may remember being scolded as a child for disturbing your mom's antiques, but imagine the wrath that ensued when unworthy subjects ostentatiously celebrated with God's fine china. A mysterious hand wrote on the wall before them and revealed Belshazzar's fate. Before the next sunrise, his empire was divided and he was killed, exactly as the writing's message foretold. Respect goes a long way with God.

These six chapters are full of bittersweet endings. We see that arrogance can lead to a path of destruction. Just remember: Pride can be a dangerous ride. However, those who were humble and given the nod from God were immensely challenged, yet they were never alone. Daniel, Shadrach, Meshach, and Abednego were confronted with potentially fatal ultimatums, but not once did their beliefs sway to match public opinion. How? There had to be some apprehension, right? I believe they were afraid initially—legs wobbly and knees knocking. Yet once their knees humbly knelt to the floor, they gained immeasurable strength and confidence to conquer any human obstacle. Here's the thing: Their love for Christ was so strong that it overcame their despair. Faith conquers fear. Their unshakable trust protected them from human harm, every single time.

Now, transport yourself to the book of Daniel. Have you ever wondered if the Alpha and Omega puts us in certain situations, merely to see how we react? How would you have responded under those same circumstances? Would you have abided by Mosaic law and denied yourself delicious spreads? As you watched a countless crowd bow down to a golden statue of another god, would you have held your stance, fully aware a fiery furnace was your destiny? Would you have possessed the resolve to continue your daily prayer in full public view, knowing good and well you would have likely been lion food by morning? Personally, I yearn for the assurance to declare a big resounding yes. At the same time, if I'm being completely honest,

I may have been Peter's clone in John 18:15–27 and let fear lead me to disassociating myself from Jesus. In present-day comparison, I strive to cling to a resolute faith and remain calm through the storms of my own life, but I have so far to go. We read that Daniel and his crew remained true to themselves and loyal to God when faced with death. Could you?

Part 2

SECOND PUZZLE EDGE: RELATIONSHIPS

Relationship: *A particular type of connection between people related to or having dealings with each other.*
—The American Heritage College Dictionary

Love is patient and kind. Love is not jealous or boastful or proud or rude. It does not demand its own way. It is not irritable, and it keeps no record of being wronged. It does not rejoice about injustice but rejoices whenever the truth wins out. Love never gives up, never loses faith, is always hopeful, and endures through every circumstance. Prophecy and speaking in unknown languages and special knowledge will become useless. But love will last forever!
—1 Corinthians 13:4–8

Chapter 5

LOVE YOUR ENEMIES

*I*magine this scenario: For months now, you have been hiding in isolation in order to escape the pandemic virus that has already consumed millions of lives. Inevitably, your emergency food supply runs out, and you must now emerge from your shelter to survive. The sun seems like a stranger, viciously blinding as it pierces your eyes. The barrenness of your surroundings becomes apparent once everything comes into focus. You are still grieving the loss of your family and friends, and from the looks of it, the sadness isn't over. Weeks, months, and even years go by as you desperately search for human contact, to no avail. The truth begins to set in: You are all alone. Initially, the world becomes your own playground. You can drive the most expensive sports cars, live in incredibly large mansions, and never have to stop at another stop sign. Can you imagine how amazing it would be to never again have to abide by those red octagons? However, you soon realize life isn't much fun if you don't have anyone to share it with. In fact, it's not worth living at all.

If you are an avid television viewer, you might recognize a similar plot in *The Last Man on Earth*. Though this sitcom is a far cry from reality, it certainly demands a new perspective. I'm sure many of us have been guilty, a time or two, of longing to crawl back into bed and pretend the rest of the world didn't exist, if only for a little while. In this previous scenario, you could live in a world without obligation, drama, or interpersonal conflict of any sort. Having the autonomy and freedom to spend your time doing whatever you desire might sound wonderful. However, as Macaulay Culkin's character eventually discovered in *Home Alone*, you should be very careful what you wish for. Because you aren't the last human on the planet and don't have the powers to make your family disappear, you must learn to coexist. The good news is, you won't have to resort to conversing with Spaldings and Wilsons; the bad news is, you still have to follow the laws of the road.

As you find your way back to reality, let this truth set in: We will foster many relationships over the course of our lifetime. *Millions* will be fleeting, with no more involvement than a quick nod or smile on the sidewalk. *Thousands* will leave their footprints through the years. *Dozens* will be the family who stand above the rest. *A handful* will steal our hearts. So I propose a question: Who is more important to treat with kindness and respect: strangers we encounter once or the familiar familial faces (say that five times fast) we consider near and dear? Our initial inkling may be closest of kin. Are we sure? What about the soul we only meet once? We never get a second chance to make a first impression. Why not treat all God's children with kindness and respect? That's what we meant to say, right?

Moments of Opportunity

Let's lock our analyzing aim onto some of the most common relationships and discuss potential, future interactions. We will begin with those transient in nature, which we may not greatly value or invest much effort in. In fact, we might not even consider these brief seconds or minutes as opportunities. We may categorize them as time wasters, in-between periods, spaces of inactivity, or downtime. Examples would be times throughout the day when we are in transition or waiting: at the coffee shop, crosswalk, grocery store, doctor's office, concession stand, city hall, DMV, post office, or any similar errand. These bouts of time in which we are waiting

for something better to happen are invaluable opportunities to be a witness. The next time you are in one of these situations and find yourself itching for the next activity or browsing your smartphone, savor the calm. Our world is so busy that going any slower than ninety miles an hour seems unusual. The problem with rushing and racing everywhere, anxiously hopping from one destination to another, or burying our faces in a cell phone, is that we lose a sense of our journey with others. When we place our attention solely on ourselves and our next endeavor, we ignore the needs of those around us. Eagerly greet the man next to you with a smile, willingly provide a listening ear to a babbling youngster, or sincerely offer encouragement to an overwhelmed mother. Your involvement doesn't have to be grandiose; simply be present and show someone you care.

Facing Opposition

Let's step our efforts up a notch. In life, we will inevitably face our fair share of opposition. Some days, people will test our limits the minute we walk out the front door. Remember that patience is a virtue (and patience doesn't hurt you), and it's one that is quickly fading. Be the exception for others to emulate. Fight the urge to dump your hot coffee on the unapologetic businessman who bumped into you because he was immersed in his phone. Harness that impulse to chuck the refund at the customer who is perturbed about a faulty product you had no control over.

You will gain awareness of your personal, mental strength when you realize your tipping point. How much emotional barrage can you withstand before your proverbial ship takes on too much water and sinks? Are you able to maintain your balance when others purposely try to rock your boat? Don't let circumstance dictate your reaction. Don't allow volatility to wreck your temperament. Whether people worship you like a king or treat you like scum between their toes, should it really affect your disposition? It's easy to reflect a smile to someone having a great day. Can you hold that same smile when they're not? Stand firm, stay true to yourself, and find rest in the safe harbor of inner peace.

Regardless of what dismay you may feel, I'm asking you to refrain from seeking revenge or telling the offending party to stick it where the sun doesn't shine. Instead, show them where it does: around you. Venture on the high road that is so seldom traveled. Don't stop there; make it a goal to bring others along as your passengers. Upon your next contact with someone unpleasant, give this experiment a shot. Kill them. Wait … did I really just say that? No need to clean your glasses or change your contacts. Kill them … with kindness.

Truth or Dare

Try this on for size. When you find your blood boiling in this kind of situation, engage yourself in a game of Truth or Dare, the one you played as a kid that brought out secrets and led to relationship firsts. This will be "Truth or Dare (well, actually just Dare): Professional Style." What better way to handle conflict than to spur competition. For those who work with the general public, challenge your coworkers for a month, and let the rest participate as judges. Here are the three dares and the corresponding scoring system for future heated confrontations. I dare you to:

1)	Ignore your initial reactions of anger and avoid retaliation	1 point
2)	Get the customer to exhibit a genuine smile	5 points
3)	Extinguish your own negativity (if unsuccessful at #2) and get the next customer to exhibit a genuine smile	2 points
	BONUS: Serve five consecutive smiling customers	3 points

Any form of verbal or physical aggression automatically disqualifies you of any points for an interaction.
The winner each month gets a free dinner from the other players.

Rather than dread the imminent exchange with an irate customer, relish the potential of adding a tally to your scorecard. While in the trenches, take five deep breaths (in through the nose and out through the mouth), and above all, remain calm. Be judicious with nonverbal communication; your body language can tell its own tale. If you have success with Dare #1, give yourself a mental pat on the back for earning one point and continue to strive for more.

Here are some helpful hints in order to achieve the highest score: Usually in these fiery bouts of frustration, we instinctually want to get the customer out of our face and out of sight as quickly as possible without causing too much of an uproar. In these situations, it's easy to tune out half the conversation—their half. Try to fight the urge to sweep the matter under the rug; rather, be engaged in the moment and use this opportunity for personal growth. Saying you're sorry is necessary but only well received if presented in the appropriate manner. From my experience, providing a robotic, apologetic response will likely only intensify the customer's fury. It's far more important to maintain sincerity, show genuine sympathy, and offer an explanation. If your response is met with unwarranted anger, you are likely a victim of transference and can shed the blame. Let me explain: An overbearing, unhappy customer may be picking up medication for her husband who was recently diagnosed with stage IV pancreatic cancer. The extended wait at your pharmacy happened to be the straw that broke the camel's, or in this case, her, back. Do your best not to take her wrath personally. In these instances, you may find that a listening ear is all you need when it becomes apparent the customer isn't actually upset with the issue at hand. This effort on your part may also help them recognize their current behavior is unjustified. Hopefully by the end of the transaction, they are appreciative of your compassion and punctuate their transformed emotion with a smile. If so, readily accept a high-five from your colleagues, tack on a handful of points, and greet the next customer with a smile.

If Dare #2 proves disastrous, and the source of your building frustration has just stormed off the scene, you are then presented the opportunity to tackle Dare #3. Shake your emotional Etch-A-Sketch, wipe away any lasting images of hostility, and extinguish possible ripple effects of negativity. Let's face it: Some people love nothing more than to spread their unhappiness wherever they go. It is empowering to know the buck stops here with you. Humbly take solace in the fact that because you endured the brunt of that anger and acted as a much-needed sounding board, steam was released. Had their rage been kept inside, it could have led to more drastic measures. Now all that's left to do is change the atmosphere by putting a smile on the next customer's face. You are on your way to earning yourself two points and, more significantly, sending positive vibes out into society.

I love competition as much as the next guy, but that's not the end goal here. I shake my head at how silly some of these suggestions are, but how often in life do we need something to nudge us into doing the right thing? Considering some of the biggest charity events, we see that many of us aren't willing to freely hand over money to help those in need; we want to know what's in it for us. What I truly hope you discover, outside of the desire to win, is how fulfilling it is to be the cause of a genuine smile.

A former colleague once shared with me how much she loved witnessing my ability to calm down unsettled patients. That was a compliment I took to heart and like to keep handy when approaching an uneasy situation. Part of my job is providing health screenings to our employees and their spouses. Here is one of my six-point success stories: One morning, a particular gentleman made everyone in his path well aware of how upset he was about having to wait for his time slot. I certainly didn't condone his behavior, although he was in for fasting lab work, and I'm the first to admit I get "hangry" on an empty stomach. Nonetheless, I kept my calm (1 point). By the end of the appointment, he was lying down on the floor and counseling me on proper yoga poses for my tight hamstrings. (If anyone has any great remedies, I'm still all ears.) He left, apologizing for his previous demeanor and donning a smile that cleared the air (5 points).

Turn the Other Cheek

Here's another angle toward understanding conflict and finding a healthy way to get revenge, without causing any harm. What really pushes an upset person's buttons? To be challenged and met with opposition? Maybe, but what I think really gets someone's goat is when he or she sees happiness across the face of an intended victim. It's human nature to want our brute force to cause visible destruction. Punching a pillow doesn't quite get the job done. We want to hear the disarray and see the chaos we voluntarily created. Color me crazy, but I believe the same logic applies with emotional conflict. The aforementioned customer expects you to crack under pressure. Don't give your challenger the satisfaction by fighting fire with fire. Instead, douse that flame with liquid love and listen to Jesus in Matthew 5:44: "But I say, love your enemies! Pray for those who persecute you!" Let the warmth of your heart overpower the steam from the hothead in front of you. We may never know what hardships the people we encounter might be battling that particular day.

Role Reversal

We should now feel confident in handling a disagreement when Mr. Irritable or Miss Sarcastic crosses our path. What about when the roles are reversed, and we become the aforementioned mister or miss? Briefly glance at the subsequent descriptors: rude, inconsiderate, and disrespectful. Have these words ever been justifiably used to describe your actions? If so, the message you conveyed to others is, "I'm really only concerned about myself. I don't have time or care enough to stop and empathize with how my behavior might be impacting those around me."

Please allow me to steal from my eight-year-old self, bantering on the playground, to help articulate my point: "Sticks and stones may break my bones, but words will never hurt me." Now, I disagree. Being on the receiving end of hurled sticks and stones may indeed result in breaks and bruises, but the human body recovers quickly. On the other hand, harsh words spewed unfiltered in the heat of the moment contain the potential to leave open wounds, lasting scars, and a lifetime of regret. Whether this next quote's origin rests with your good ol' mom or Thumper from the childhood classic *Bambi*, let the lesson sink in: "If you can't say something nice, don't say nothing at all." (While Bambi struggled learning how to walk, Thumper needed help with his grammar.) Taking deep breaths and slowly counting to ten in these heated moments may provide us ample time to mellow, think better on the matter, and prevent detonating verbal explosives.

My intentions in writing this book weren't to condemn all our actions and criticize our every move, yet I hope we feel remorse when we speak out of line with negative connotation. I am not naïve enough to believe we will be a constant, or even daily, ray of sunshine going forward. There will inevitably be "Mondays" when we wake up on the wrong side of the bed; I certainly have experienced my fair share. With that being said, just like yawning is contagious (someone still needs to explain this phenomenon to me), unrivaled pessimism can quickly ignite nearby victims and ultimately run rampant throughout the community. We as individuals are not fully aware of the powerful potential we possess to negatively or positively impact the people we see every day. We merely need to decide if we want to make or break someone's day. Thankfully, you can still "make" even after you "break," as my coworkers have learned.

Emotional Roller Coaster

The majority of our customers are exceptionally courteous, but just like any position with direct customer involvement, our pharmacy staff withstands a fair share of verbal punishment from the public. Rather than focus on the hundreds of pleasantries we are fortunate to experience, we always seem to hold onto that one negative encounter. A particular incident from years ago comes to mind: A patient of ours became disgruntled over a pending prescription, quickly voiced his unhappiness, and then sped out of the drive-thru. Our employee on the receiving end personally knew this man and was quite upset from his comments. A couple of minutes ticked by, and I saw tears stream down her face as she hung up the phone. That same belligerent patient had called back. Upon recognizing his voice, our employee again apologized about the issue that had caused his irritation, but the man silenced her midsentence and in a hushed tone said, "I don't care about my prescription; I care that I hurt you, and I'm very sorry for that."

What a range of emotions she cycled through in such a brief timespan. This story is a rare exception to how these scenarios normally unfold. I consider myself fortunate to have had a first-row seat to such a moment, which confirmed that no matter how crazy the world may seem, goodness still remains at humanity's core. You never can predict what the good Lord will send your way when you wake up for the day; that, my friends, is what keeps life interesting.

Learn Humility

Throughout your journey, you will encounter all walks of life. Remember this: Never be too good for someone else. My uncle, whose comic genius could have you laughing at a funeral, recently extended his art-teaching skills from the classroom to the streets. His passion and willingness to reach out to the common man was put on display when he provided supplies and offered free lessons to the local homeless community. Occupation, socioeconomic status, gender, race, age, or any other discriminating factor should not determine our level of compassion.

What a powerful reminder that statement is for me. There isn't a special playbook on how to interact with others, but we can and should all live by the Golden Rule. In Matthew 7:12, Jesus instructs us, "Do to others whatever you would like them to do to you. This is the essence of all that is taught in the law and the prophets." Wouldn't that quickly eliminate hatred, violence, and contempt? Next time your nostrils flare, eyes bulge, and veins pop out of your forehead, simmer down. Then picture yourself on the other side, as if that green, Hulk-like rage of fury was headed for you. As I mentioned earlier, anger is often a transferred emotion from a previous incident. Why voice your displeasure at someone who isn't the source? People don't deserve that treatment. Forget finding a solution; you are creating another problem. Mathematicians assert that two negatives make a positive; however, that line of reasoning doesn't spill over into social behaviors. If we collectively work to lose the negativity, we are sure to exponentially increase the positivity throughout the world.

Chapter 6

LOVING LOVED ONES

All right, so now that we can appreciate how to treat the John Smiths and Jane Does we encounter, what about our favorite people we couldn't imagine living a single day without? Remember the opening question from the previous chapter: Who is more important to treat with kindness and respect: strangers you encounter once or your parent, spouse, sibling, child, or BFF? If you answered the latter, do you in fact selflessly serve those people? Or, more often than not, must you bashfully admit to participating in spouting these instigating verbal grenades?

Scenario One

"Hi, honey, you didn't tell me you were going to get home so late *again*."

"I had to finish up some things that took longer than I thought. *Okay?*"

"I wish you would have called."

"I was too busy."

"Well, we've been waiting on you for over two hours now."

And on it goes …

Scenario Two

"I'm looking forward to a relaxing night tomorrow."

"Uh ... that won't be tomorrow night. We have parent-teacher conferences."

"We do? You could have told me about this *earlier.*"

"Sweetheart, we talked about this last week. I swear you *never* listen."

Boy, don't we hate hearing those words?

Scenario Three

"Ugh, this kitchen is *always* such a mess."

"Sorry, I was running late this morning and didn't have a chance to clean up."

"Rinsing your bowl and putting it in the dishwasher *only* takes a few seconds."

"I didn't have a few seconds this morning, dear. I was busy cleaning up after the dog because *you* left him out again."

Boom: fight on ...

Do our actions match our intentions? Would we yell at our teacher for running late to class or scold our boss for not listening? Do we bark at our roommate for not keeping the kitchen nice and tidy? We probably hold our true feelings inside and keep them to ourselves to avoid offending anyone. However, when it comes to those we say we love the most, all bets are off, and the filter is impulsively ripped away. Am I implying we ought to treat others with the same brutal honesty we do our loved ones? No, not necessarily, because there is a sense of openness and vulnerability with that level of intimacy. But isn't it funny how we don't hold anything back from our closest companions when it comes to expressing our unhappiness? As the scenarios demonstrated, we grow impatient toward repeated tardiness from work. We speak in a condescending tone when previous conversations are forgotten. We harp about dishes constantly piled up in the sink. Sound familiar? Guilty as charged for me, on all three occasions.

Transference

Perhaps your arguments don't follow this exact pattern, but you probably have your own repetitive quarrels. I would be willing to bet the results are the same. To better understand the issue at hand, let's revisit the concept of transference we briefly discussed earlier. Who are we most likely to transfer our negative attitude onto after a lousy day on the job or a rough afternoon at home with the kids? The answer is often the unfortunate souls within earshot.

Suppose after a great day apart, we find ourselves at home in the middle of those same three scenarios. Would our brash questioning and responses be altered in any way? I believe so. The message may hold a similar meaning, but the tone and use of offensive or defensive language, such as placing blame and adding absolutes, would likely be appreciably different. This transformation of exchanges implies that the actual source of our frustration is not the innocent party we just verbally attacked, but rather the stressors of the day we unknowingly carried into the conversation. Being able to leave our problems outside the front door can prevent us from entering into unnecessary marital battles. (Check yourself before you wreck yourself.) Now, instead of World War III ensuing each night in the household, with our counterparts seemingly walking through a field of landmines, we can learn to disarm the artillery, leave the drama behind, and enjoy the rest of our evening.

If, however, you are welcomed home with remarks that transform your sunshine of a day into an emotional thunderstorm, then perhaps it's time to have a healthy confrontation. I realize these two words often have a hard time coexisting; a lot of people hate the latter, but I believe it's because they leave out the former. Every strong relationship needs, and requires, some form of confrontation. Denial of this statement should raise a red flag you need to quickly address. I'm not a marriage counselor, but I would be remiss if I didn't offer my two cents. I've gained much from great resources along my marital journey.

Go Get the Emotional Plunger

Now, what are some ways we can improve that special bond with our one and only? Where do we start? I know, I know, pick me (hand raised). Communication. Open up the lines. If you only remember one paragraph in this chapter, let it be this one. Communication is absolutely essential to a successful and fulfilling relationship. Don't assume; talk. My wife and I don't fight very often, but when we have disagreements that are not a result of just being "hangry," nine times out of ten, they are due to a lack of communication or misinterpretation. Recognize your clog. I bet you would find similar statistics across the board of relationships if you investigated further. Five minutes a day of focused dialogue, rather than monologue, can be the difference between decades of lasting happiness and slowly growing further apart, day by day.

The key to positive, and therefore successful, communication is making sure your message isn't received as another "c" word: complaining or criticizing. Try to explain your displeasure for a particular situation, rather than assigning blame. If you are victorious in leaving fault at the door, you will have accomplished your mission of capturing your audience. Ears will start to close and mouths will quickly open when others feel attacked or threatened. The longer their lips are zipped, the greater chance you have of being heard. Now you can get down to business and carefully share your concerns.

Once the emotional burden is off your chest, graciously reciprocate in relieving your significant other of his or her angst. Give each other undivided attention when voicing your respective opinions. Let the one talking hold the imaginary key to unlock the other's mouth when finished, and only then. Putting yourself in each other's shoes as you digest the information may offer another perspective and even teach you a lesson or two. Regardless of any personal benefit, tuning in will at the very least give your partner a feeling of importance; that in itself will have been worth your efforts. After all, you may be amazed by what you hear and learn when you take the time to dialogue. God brilliantly designed us with ears (plural) and a mouth (singular). You will be all the more wise if you focus on the pair and not the one. As the book of James so concisely advises, "Understand this, my dear brothers and sisters: You must all be quick to listen, slow to speak, and slow to get angry" (1:19). Remember: Healthy confrontation means all voices are heard, especially those that may feel insignificant. Otherwise, repetitive silence may result in submissiveness. Submissiveness may then lead to resentment. And over time, resentment has the potential to destroy a relationship.

Meet the Parrotts

An excellent resource that has helped improve our marriage was a presentation my wife and I attended called "Fight Night," by husband-and-wife psychologist team, Les and Leslie Parrott. This highly entertaining power couple explained why conflict occurs in the first place and offered solutions for how to have healthy conflict. More information can be found on their website, www.lesandleslie. com, should you choose to take advantage of their marital wisdom.

In with the Glad

When getting ready to receive good and bad news, which do you want first? My wife and I often ask each other this question when debriefing our day. My answer is like clockwork; I always choose to get the bad news out of the way so I can rest on the good. That's what I attempted in formatting this section. As we discussed conflict and areas for improvement, we have no doubt discovered the flaws and weaknesses of ourselves, as well as our counterpart. I'm guessing these weren't the reasons you started dating in the first place. Moving on, it's out with the bad and sad and mad—and in with the glad.

Shout-Out to *The 5 Love Languages*

While I'm sure there are countless resources available today, another one I passionately recommend is *The 5 Love Languages* by Gary

Chapman. You will learn that there are five basic ways to express and receive love. The languages are as follows:

1. **Words of Affirmation**: verbal compliments, statements of affection and appreciation, or encouraging words
2. **Quality Time**: giving of undivided attention
3. **Receiving Gifts**: tangible and visual symbols
4. **Acts of Service**: genuine actions or tasks
5. **Physical Touch**: any form of physical intimacy

The fundamental principle to grasp when reading this treasure is to discover which of the five your significant other primarily speaks. Then, of equal importance, is to demonstrate your newfound awareness by learning to converse in their language and fill their love tank.

Less for You, More for Them

Regardless of the resources you utilize to improve your relationship, remember this: Solutions are often simple to understand but difficult to implement, because they demand selflessness. You must decide that your happiness is no longer your major concern. Making sacrifices to plant a smile on your partner's face will hopefully become your new primary goal. Girls, you may decide to give up buying those pink high heels. Guys, you might find yourself at the ballet. Changes to your regular routine may take some time to get used to, but wait and see how your relationship will be all the better for it in the end, and much, much stronger. Selfish pleasures don't hold a candle to the absolute joy you will experience when you recognize you are the responsible party for the heartfelt smile across the room.

Chapter 7

MY HEAVEN ON EARTH

My Profession of Love

*A*h, how great it is to reminisce about the budding stages of a relationship. Try to recall all the excitement that occurred: butterflies in the stomach, practicing his last name on paper (yes, we saw you girls), sleepless nights of running on pure adrenaline, puppy love, and PDA that brought nausea to innocent bystanders. What was it about him or her that made you take that leap of faith? In describing your significant other to family and friends, what characteristics come to mind? As you compile your list, let me introduce you to the love of my life: my wife, Holly.

Holly is and will always be the most beautiful woman in my eyes, inside and out, both consciously and subconsciously. What do I mean by "subconsciously"? During shopping excursions together, we occasionally part ways. As we are separated, I inevitably begin to people watch. On one particular occasion, as I was in my study of deep observation, I caught an initial glance of an attractive woman gliding in my direction who piqued my curiosity. After a few seconds passed, I took that second, forbidden look. (I'm a married man, so I realize I may be digging my own grave with this confession.) It was obvious—her smile was targeted at me. Then I realized her true identity. This alluring, untouchable woman was in fact my incredibly captivating wife.

Why do I publicly share this moment of involuntary, animalistic attraction, knowing very well I could be sleeping on the couch tonight? I've got my reasons. The universal response for any man or woman when asked, "Who is the most attractive individual?" should be his or her one and only, or they risk joining me in the doghouse. My point is that I noticed my wife's beauty outside of those biased glasses. That gives me confirmation that our chemistry is real. This happenstance has actually occurred more than once.

I will continue my fondness. Holly possesses the power to illuminate a room when she flashes her pearly whites; as a result, she has rightfully earned the nickname "Smiley" by some. Her sense of humor is contagious, and it frequently leaves me chuckling. Life is too short to be serious all the time, and our playful banter certainly supports this position. Attending a Women of Faith conference reignited Holly's spiritual journey. This, in turn, led her to join a Bible study, anxiously dig into God's word, and re-examine what she truly believes. She continues to strengthen her faith and accelerate her walk with Christ, which means *our* faith is deepening.

Her newest role as mother has given me a whole new sense of appreciation. Twice now, I have been inspired by the mental strength Holly embodied throughout her all-day sickness over the eighteen months of her pregnancies. Despite a constant green hue of uneasiness, her pregnancy glow was still radiant and ever-present. I witnessed a true dying of self, as the care for her needs became secondary to those of our miracles growing inside. Months later, patience was actively defined when I stood in awe of her unwavering gentleness during bouts of incessant wailing. From a vivacious girlfriend, promising fiancée, devoted wife, and now a nurturing mother of my children, there isn't a stage of life I want to spend without her.

I believe the best part of our relationship is our ability to do nothing and be perfectly content. When our family calendar is empty of engagements, boredom never sets in. We don't need to catch a sporting event or concert to be energized. Don't get me wrong: We enjoy our time out as much as the next couple, but for those who are always on the go, ask yourself this question: What do you enjoy more, the entertainment or the person you are enjoying it with? There may come a day when you are both in your nineties (either ninety years old or ninety years young—you choose) and a trip to the mailbox will constitute as an excursion. Have you chosen the right person to be rocking on the front porch beside?

If you personally know my wife and my corresponding adoration, you would agree I could go on and on, testifying to her amazing qualities. In case I have lost you and led you to believe we live in a magical fairytale, she is also a hot mess, scatterbrained, unorganized, the opposite of punctual, and one who sneezes really unexpectedly and violently. With all that being said, I choose to focus on her positives. Included in those positives are how she makes me want to be a better person in every way. I still can't believe out of all the men in this world, she chose me. To say I feel grateful is an understatement. Some people dream of winning the lottery. I personally will sacrifice the monetary reward in exchange for the overflowing fulfillment of living with a woman who makes my dreams come true every single day (cue nausea, right?). In the words of Leo Christopher, "I swear I couldn't love you more than I do right now, and yet I know I will tomorrow." When you find *her* (or *him*), it will all make sense.

What about Your Better Half?

If you are in a relationship, are you able to share a similar list of your one and only when you reflect on the wonderful spice he or she adds to your life? Do you make your spouse a priority? Do you show your significant other how much you care? Borrowing from the cofounder of the Methodist Church, John Wesley: Do you love them by all the means you can, in all the ways you can, in all the places you can, at all the times you can, for as long as ever you can? Don't ever take what you have, or more meaningfully, *who* you have by your side, for granted. This basic notion has hit very close to home in the past couple years. Too many tears have been shed for the lives lost within

my coworkers' families. Seeing all the hurt and pain on their faces during times of tragedy reminds me that my daily mishaps are trivial. Amazingly, all my worries seem to fade away the moment I get home, the garage door opens, and I see who is awaiting me.

Now that we have hopefully reached a consensus that we need to treat the objects of our affection better, let's look at how we can do just that. Perception is crucial. You may have heard that in all relationships, one person is the "reacher" and the other the "settler." My wife and I both honestly believe we are the former. Strive to be the one who marries up, at least in your eyes. Through those admiring goggles, your spouse will steadily inspire you to be the best version of yourself. And when you wake up every morning knowing you struck matrimonial gold, do your best to treat that person like the queen (or king) they are, 365 days of the year.

Let's talk about one particular day, February 14, for a minute. Valentine's Day is a wonderful time to remember and celebrate your love, not a magical redemption period. Those twenty-four hours shouldn't be used as an out for being inadequate the other 364 days of the year. With a few quick swipes of plastic, many in the doghouse annually buy their special someone apologetic flowers, jewelry, and chocolates. Fellas, you don't need a special day of expectations for wining, dining, and commemorating your relationship. Make those sentiments last beyond the holiday, and cherish your soulmates every day. Freely and regularly shower them with "just because" gestures that will warm their hearts. And regardless of what stage your relationship is in—just beginning, fresh off a honeymoon, or celebrating 50 years together—don't forget to keep dating. Never get complacent; always keep the love alive.

Party of One

For those who shed a tear over not being able to check "plus one" on a wedding invitation, take heart. You are not alone, and time is certainly not passing you by. Jealousy of the rings, babies, and lifelong love all your friends seem to be enjoying isn't productive. Celebrate their joy. In the same breath, find comfort in your situation. There is a reason for this particular season in your life. Appreciate where you are and what you have, rather than focusing on what's missing.

If you are anxiously waiting for love to come and slap you in the face, trust in the bigger picture. Too many times, the feelings of unanswered prayers leave us weary with uncertainty. When we don't experience the fruition of our prayers, we may wonder if we have God's ears. God is the writer, director, and producer. He is casting the roles and working diligently behind the scenes in the movie of your life, yet to be released. He will deliver the costar of your dreams, and rest assured He will guide you both in the right direction. It's in our human nature to assume we know what's best. But our Creator is just that—the One Who created the heavens and the earth, and we are only a tiny morsel within. Have faith knowing God has your best interest at heart. Don't fret, and when you start to feel like your worries aren't under His care, don't forget Luke 12:6–7: "What is the price of five sparrows—two copper coins? Yet God does not forget a single one of them. And the very hairs on your head are all numbered. So don't be afraid; you are more valuable to God than a whole flock of sparrows."

As for those of you in your teenage years, rejection is admittedly hard when your feelings aren't reciprocated. I know; I've been there. First, I want you to know your life isn't over; it's just beginning. Do not let middle or high school define you. Use the disappointments for growth and the successes as encouragement in the direction of personal development. A lifetime of opportunity awaits you. Second, ask yourself the question I would also pose to the lovely ladies who don't receive a rose as they vie for the attention of one man on the reality show *The Bachelor*: "Why would you want to be with a man who doesn't desire you?" I have told many of my female friends who are still on the hunt for Mr. Right, "Don't settle for a man who says he can live with you; only accept a hand from the one who admits he can't live without you."

Exercise patience, improve yourself, and trust in God. Girls, your knight in shining armor will arrive right on time (His, not yours).

Guys, the woman of your dreams will cross your path at just the right moment. When love finds you, don't lose your identity or forget the rest of the world around you. I wholeheartedly confess my own weakness of allowing family and good friends to temporarily slip to the back burner at times. Show those who are close to you that you still recognize how preciously God-given they are.

Many of you may go through life with God leading you in a different direction. Not all of us are called to be a husband or wife, mom or dad. Ask any priest about their discernment. Outside of building a family or standing behind a pulpit, God might place your focus and commitment elsewhere; it's up to you to find it. Regardless of your calling, your relationship with God should be prioritized above all. As you search for yourself, focus on Matthew 6:33: "Seek the Kingdom of God above all else, and live righteously, and he will give you everything you need."

My Testimonial—As a Brother

Up to this point, I have highlighted certain relationships in my life. I have described how grateful I am for my parents and the woman I proudly call my wife. I would be remiss if I didn't articulate how amazing my two sisters are. Yes, siblings are included as part of the familiar familial faces we should treat with kindness and respect every day. I will admit, my relationship is different with each of the two.

Megan

My middle sister, Megan, is only three years younger, and we grew up right alongside each other. We had our fair share of fights, no doubt, but isn't that a love language in those younger years? Honestly, though, to this day, my mom reminds me time and time again, and it's so true it bears repeating: Megan was so selfless and always thought of her big brother. Whenever she was given a cookie, she never left without a second one for me in hand.

That selfless nature is something she hasn't lost; in fact, it has only gotten stronger through her maturation. After watching the movie *The Giver*, I now have the perfect compliment. In this particular film, all emotions were abolished from the community because of society's overwhelming hatred and violence. I am fully convinced intervention wouldn't have been necessary if clones of Megan were the only humans in existence. She is without a doubt one of the most genuine people I know.

Whether baking delicious desserts, crocheting newborn blankets, or purchasing the perfect "just because" memento, she has earned the title the *Gift Whisperer*. She always seems to possess an inclination of what others need at just the right moment. While we live in a "me" generation, Megan stands out among the crowd for her compassion and thoughtfulness. God is ever-present in her life, and I believe He uses her as a fine-tuned instrument to demonstrate what it means to be a devoted Christian, day in and day out. She truly defines this great quote from Maya Angelou: "A woman's heart must be so hidden in God that a man has to seek Him to find her."

Morgan

My other sister, Morgan, is the baby of our family, making her royal entrance ten years later. Because of the vast age difference, we always lovingly joked about her growing up with four parents. I will never forget the day she was born and the excitement she brought to our world. Holding her in my arms and rocking her to sleep that first night as her big brother was indescribable. She captured our attention from day one. We hung onto every goo, ga, and innocent gummy grin that emanated from her angelic face. Lapping up milk from a glass with her tongue was a hilarious spectacle for all of us. My mom said I used to love imitating her babbling sounds and having intimate nightly conversations at the crib.

As I have since moved from the house that built me (a la Miranda Lambert) and out of the town I proudly roamed for twenty-two years, I am sadly left to watch her grow 'from afar. Giving the latest and greatest technology a bad rap is something I'm guilty of, but I have to say that it has certainly been monumental for us in staying close. She does her best to keep me current and in the know. I'm only thirty-two and already falling out of the loop on what's considered cool (though I'm not sure I ever really knew). I greatly admire her moxie and the no-fear mentality she has adopted. Morgan lives with the confidence I wish I owned. I'm still not sure where life is going to take her, but one thing is for sure: She is destined for greatness. I am so incredibly proud of my two sisters for the women they have become.

The Outlaws

My blessings only continued to multiply when I was fortunate enough to marry into the Parry family. My father-in-law, Dennis, is the epitome of a hard-working American: a true labor-of-love kind of guy. We often joke about how he only works half a day; the other twelve hours, he steps away from his food market. My mother-in-law, Linda, our beloved "Granny Nanny", spreads kindness and generosity without boundaries. She is also one of the most creative spirits alive. Their two other daughters amaze me in their respective ways. Mindy Mae, Holly's older clone and one of the responsible parties for Paisley's middle name, is one of my favorite people in this world—no explanation necessary. Hang out with her for a quick minute, and you will surely wish for all your days to include a little bit of Min. The eldest, my partner in crime on being the oldest sibling, Jill, has shown me as a first-time parent what love for a child looks like. Her precious firecracker of a daughter, Adelyn, was born a little over a year before Paisley, and we happily accept hand-me-downs and foreshadowing of all the upcoming developmental landmarks. Stemming from immediate family, I also must avow that I have been privileged to be surrounded by a wonderful cast of grandparents, uncles, aunts, and cousins. What about you? Do you let each of your loved ones know how much they mean to you?

Chapter 8

FRIENDS ARE THE
FAMILY WE CHOOSE

*O*utside of your family and friends, you may not value or put forth much effort to impress those acquaintances transient in nature. Here's my question: How can you predict which ones will be transient? I have to believe you can't. Remember that your best friends were once strangers. Those initial greetings likely didn't foretell countless years of camaraderie. Treat everyone with kindness and respect, and watch who God brings into your life to stay.

Scott

Friends are the family we choose, and I have certainly hit the jackpot. Immerse yourself in the graces of good company, and you can't go wrong. There are countless examples I could share, but I will settle with a couple of the most recent. My friends and family threw me an early surprise birthday party for my big 3-0. My sister (remember, the *Gift Whisperer*) instinctively understands my love for inspirational words of wisdom. She instructed all attendees to bring their favorite quote and used them collectively to construct an amazing scrapbook. While everyone else inked their heartfelt favorites, Scott, the best man at our wedding and my best friend to this day, went one step further (like he often does). In between training for marathons, teaching, and coaching, he put his artistic prowess on display and cross-stitched Isaiah 40:31: "But those who trust in the Lord will find new strength. They will soar high on wings like eagles. They will run and not grow weary. They will walk and not faint."

Holly and I are counting on Scott to be an instrumental influence in the lives of our daughter and son. He got a great start by driving several hours to be part of Paisley's baby dedication ceremony and starting collections of Dr. Seuss books and *Sports Illustrated* magazines for Paisley and Lucas, respectively. In addition, as part of his self-imposed duty as best man, he gave me a reminder call the night before my first wedding anniversary. At the pinnacle of my fondest memories with Scott are our midnight filibuster-worthy driveway conversations throughout our phases of life. His words always seem to hit me at my core, leaving me eternally grateful to God for giving me a best friend who truly understands me.

Nick

One of my groomsmen and best friends, Nick, is a walking miracle after a face-to-face encounter with death. (Stay tuned for the rest of his story.) He has traveled around the country to share his story and proclaim the love of God. One of his speaking engagements was at the church where Holly and I recited our vows. During Nick's testimonial, he mentioned that our wedding was held there and that we were expecting. He proceeded to lead the congregation in a prayer for the health and safety of our forthcoming baby girl. Months later, he brought my wife and me to tears when he mailed Paisley a handwritten letter describing the impact of his relationship with her dad.

Nick also snatched me a ticket to game six of the 2014 World Series. And he's the one who encouraged me to face my fear, as we went up the hundred-foot-tall Skycoaster during my bachelor party. To outdo himself, upon his trip from the Holy Land, he gave us rosaries that had touched the foot of the cross. We all have that one person in life who continually inspires and challenges us every step of the way; he's definitely mine. Nick makes me a better man in all walks of life.

Spoiled by Good Company

From receiving a homemade card and lots of spoiling from coworkers on my birthday to being instantly presented with a fun-filled itinerary each time we arrive at our friends' home to watching my sister-in-law go all out for family holiday parties to greeting a friend of mine in a traditional chest-bumping fashion at every encounter to having a neighboring friend on speed-dial who would always give you the shirt off his back (as well as anything else you'd need) to having friends go through multiple trash sacks at a fast food restaurant looking for our lost credit card to witnessing a Christian brother visit the local hospital chapel solely to pray for my dad in surgery to enjoying a lasting friendship that started just outside the womb—I am in the presence of some pretty incredible people. Our time always lacks in quantity but is compensated by quality. I sincerely hope you have countless memorable tales you can share about the wondrous company around you.

Are You Doing Your Part?

Now conversely, return the favor and be actively and forever present for your family and friends. Surprise your best friend in Boston to watch him run the marathon. Take a personal day from work to spend quality time with a friend who is leaving town. Make a goal to be a best man or maid of honor, symbolizing your impact on another's life. It is such an honor to stand as a right-hand man as you help a friend celebrate the best day of his life. I personally accepted this privilege on the sands of the Bahamas, and that was a truly rewarding experience.

Whether a brief moment on a busy street corner, a thirty-second encounter at work, a blossoming friendship, or a loving marriage—all of these relationships are important. As Robert Louis Stevenson wisely advised, "Don't judge each day by the harvest you reap, but by the seeds you plant." Some gestures may seem small and insignificant to you, but that smile or random act of kindness may mean everything to the recipient. It may be only one of the thousands of days you are privileged to live here, but those twenty-four hours matter. In one of those 1,440 minutes, wouldn't it be magical to know you changed someone's life forever? Strive to leave a positive imprint wherever your soles touch the pavement. In order to do so, you can ill afford to have an off-day. You never know who or what will come your way or when that day may occur. Suppress the coasting mind-set and remain alert for opportunities that arise. Those moments are often invisible for people clouding their mental capacity with selfish desires. In the words of JFK, our highly regarded late president, "My fellow Americans, ask not what your country can do for you; ask what you can do for your country." Perceive the world as your playground to make a difference.

Chapter 9

FROM THE LIVING WORD: RUTH'S SACRIFICIAL LOVE

Throughout the Bible, you will uncover many different types of relationships. Let's turn our focus to a book found early in the Old Testament: Ruth. Women played a more submissive role in the early church of the Old Testament; they were often expected to sit in silence, much like children of that day. So for a book to be named after a woman (the only other being Esther, who is partly responsible for this book's subtitle), you can gather she was no ordinary woman. The book of Ruth is only a short four-chapter narrative, but there are considerable lessons to be learned, and an enormous amount of material we all need to take to heart.

Allow me to quickly set the stage: Elimelech and Naomi were an Israelite couple who had two sons, Mahlon and Kilion. There was a famine in their homeland of Israel, which forced them to go to the undesirable city of Moab. While in Moab, Elimelech passed away, and the sons met and married two Moabite women, named Orpah and Ruth. A decade later, Mahlon and Kilion both perished, leaving Naomi in the company of her two daughters-in-law. Shortly after, there was word God had ended the famine, so the three women packed up in preparation for the journey back to Israel. In that moment, Naomi realized it was unfair to expect the girls to accompany her. She thanked them for their years together, but explained there was no more she could do for them. Blessing them, she insisted they stay with their families. Orpah initially disagreed with Naomi's request, but with a little convincing, she decided to stay in Moab.

Ruth's response showed her altruistic character and unveiled her unwavering loyalty to Naomi: "But Ruth replied, 'Don't ask me to leave you and turn back. Wherever you go, I will go; wherever you live, I will live. Your people will be my people, and your God will be my God. Wherever you die, I will die, and there I will be buried. May the Lord punish me severely if I allow anything but death to separate us!'" (Ruth 1:16-17)

To fully understand and appreciate these words, let us recap Ruth's situation: She had just buried her husband of ten years and was faced with the difficult decision between staying in Moab with her family and following her mother-in-law to a foreign land. Her sister, by marriage, had already made the logical decision to return to her birth family. Why would Ruth kiss her family good-bye and freely give up all she had ever known? What did she have to gain? Naomi even admitted there wasn't anything left for her to offer in return. Ruth's future consisted of shadowing a woman who had blamed God for their recent tragedies, causing her to lose her faith and become so pessimistic that she changed her name from Naomi (meaning "pleasant") to Mara (meaning "bitter").

Let's put ourselves in Ruth's predicament and try to rationalize her path of decision-making. Her attitude was unusual at the time, but today, we might even consider her a little crazy. We live in a "me" generation, and I believe the majority of us would expect to be consoled after losing a spouse, rather than be the one to console. Self-pity would likely creep in and eventually consume our inner thoughts, clouding our ability to turn our focus toward others. Ruth possessed a rare spiritual strength that allowed her to suppress her own grief in order to provide comfort and support for a heart-stricken Naomi. In a life with little promise, God provided Ruth with the light to see the next step and instilled in her the courage to take it.

As we continue reading, a love story begins to unfold. Ruth sought out work according to Naomi's instruction, which found her working in the field of an older man named Boaz. Boaz was a well-to-do yet genuine man who treated everyone he encountered with a special kindness. He instantly took a liking to Ruth. Boaz was deeply moved when he learned of her past, and as a result, he allowed her to continue collecting from his grains. Throughout the days ahead, Ruth carried out specific instructions given to her from Naomi, who had encouraged her to pursue an interest in Boaz. The blossoming relationship of Boaz and Ruth actually transformed the heart of Naomi and restored her faith in God. Her bitterness withered, and her pleasant nature re-emerged. The future happiness of her daughter-in-law became her utmost priority, as she coached Ruth into finding favor in the eyes of Boaz. Naomi advised Ruth to wash, perfume, and dress in her Sunday best one night during the harvest. Ruth presented herself on the threshing floor (where the grain is separated from the straw and husks) in a different light to symbolize to Boaz she welcomed the idea of a marriage together. I suppose you could cue the lights, camera, and action; this was likely the night they fell in love.

Turning the pages, we also discover Boaz to be Mahlon's kinsman-redeemer, a term in Mosaic law that was put in place to rescue a widow and her property. After the nearest of kin refused his rights, Boaz agreed to buy Mahlon's property and make Ruth his wife. And so the saying goes, they lived happily ever after. The newly married couple bore a son named Obed, and from him came Jesse, who fathered the famous King David, whose lineage ultimately led to Christ Jesus.

This lesson-packed love story in the Old Testament is a shining reminder that God sees your heart and is always watching. From an outside perspective, Ruth's life was nothing more than a dead end. Unbeknownst to us, the Director was merely changing scenery for the beginning of a beautiful road ahead. Because of her unfailing loyalty, God showed His steadfast love.

We have discussed quite a mixed bag of relationships over these last few chapters, but they all should hold a universal theme in our souls. When you offer yourself up and invest in God's graces to spread His love, you can revel in the amazing amount of return. It's far better to give than to receive. How many times have we heard this? The incredible feeling that overtakes you when bringing others happiness is second to none. This was no doubt God's intention and well-constructed design to reward His humble and faithful servants. Isn't He awesome?

Part 3

THIRD PUZZLE EDGE: VOCATION

Vocation: *A regular occupation, esp. one for which
a person is particularly suited or qualified.*
—The American Heritage College Dictionary

*So, my dear brothers and sisters, be strong and immovable.
Always work enthusiastically for the Lord, for you know
that nothing you do for the Lord is ever useless.*
—1 Corinthians 15:58

Chapter 10

HAPPINESS IN THE WORKPLACE

$\mathscr{I}$ sincerely hope we now have a newfound appreciation for relationships, because they are all special in their own ways. Of the many different types of people we interact with, who do we spend the most time with on a daily basis? Our immediate response is probably our families, but let's take a minute to reconsider and discover the truth. There are twenty-four hours in a day, no matter how many more we try to cram in there—always twenty-four. For simplicity's sake, let's break down a weekday into three equal eight-hour periods. Assuming we follow general standards of health and hold a full-time job, we spend eight hours asleep and eight hours on the working clock. The remaining hours can be used as we please.

Splitting the day into three equal sections is optimal for our discussion. However, if we are realistic, the scales are likely tipped toward working for the man. Many spend nine, ten, or even more hours on the job—and that's not including the commute. Then, ironically, we work hard to accumulate seven or eight hours of restful shut-eye. That leaves us approximately eight hours left in the day, which quickly fill up with errands, household chores, general hygiene, exercise, nutrition, and other daily demands.

Recall the question at hand: Who do we spend the most time with on a daily basis? I think we can all agree that hours spent catching z's don't amount to quality time with anyone, so that time is out of the running. As for our miscellaneous freedom off the clock, I would venture to guess we are here, there, and everywhere—not necessarily in the same continual company. That leaves … drum roll, please … our fellow employees to claim the trophy. It may be a hard pill to swallow when we realize that we see more of our colleagues than our loved ones. Therefore, since we spend so much time working, finding that perfect job is important.

So how do we find the *perfect* job? I laugh at this word, as I presume many of us do, when the word "job" immediately follows. For most people, this combination simply doesn't exist. In that case, maybe our job search shouldn't be for perfection but rather happiness.

How do we achieve happiness for all eight hours a day, five days a week, fifty weeks a year (assuming we have compiled at least two weeks of vacation)? Pessimists say we won't, and I won't lie to you— they are right. There will be hours, days, weeks, months, and possibly even years where we desire to be anywhere but work. Be that as it may, fellow optimists and I say striving for anything less sets us up for failure. When shooting a basketball, we know we won't make every shot. However, the belief in the potential of each attempt is the best way to achieve consistent success. Apply the same philosophy at your workplace, and approach each day like it will be your best one yet.

We aren't all at the same stop in our professional journeys. Are you still in high school? Did you recently apply for college? Are you on the verge of landing your first job? Have you been with the same company for the better part of a decade? No matter where we are at in life, there is always room for betterment. We give ourselves the best chance for professional success by gaining a sound education, so let's start there.

Advice for New Graduates

Some of you may have recently graduated high school, previously just another small fish in the big high school sea. You likely enrolled in classes that, for the most part, were predetermined according to a specific curriculum. Well, guess what: You are now the fisherman, meaning you get to choose the open body of water where you take your rod and reel. Before you hastily or carelessly cast your collegiate line, learn from others' past regrets. My college advisor once shared that only 10 percent of graduates actually end up in an occupation pertaining to their degrees. Isn't that percentage staggering? Doesn't it provide even more reason to choose your path wisely and take your higher education seriously? Be a part of the 10 percent. Investing in college (while I realize it's not for everyone) will be one of the most significant decisions you make in life, so make the right one.

Deciding on a career can be a formidable task. Let go of the overwhelming fear of uncertainty. Start simply by taking a personality test to systematically uncover your strengths and weaknesses to see where you fall on the map: introvert versus extrovert, sensing versus intuition, thinking versus feeling, judging versus perceiving. By no means is this quiz a be-all and end-all solution, but this method does offer an initial stepping-stone. Your results on paper might not necessarily align with your preliminary career prospects, so do your homework and analyze all angles.

Another hidden clue for discovering your niche is to detect an area where you excel: your competitive advantage. What abilities do others struggle with that you are able to effortlessly maneuver? That unique proficiency may lend insight to where you should land your focus. These various approaches may lead to an overwhelming number of options. You may find yourself draining the ink from your pen as you cross out one category after the next. The silver lining is that your hand-eye coordination and, in turn, basketball skills may significantly improve from repetitively shooting crumpled paper into the circular file. Be patient through this brainstorming phase, because all those frustrating times you say, "no" can help expose the culminating *yes*.

Take advantage of having guidance counselors or advisors at your disposal, and allow them to help you hone in on plausible career options. As you narrow your selections, experiment with different avenues by shadowing experts in their respective trades. Don't let one day determine absolutes in various fields, but take these opportunities for what they are: a peek inside the profession. Continue to explore and practice your craft in areas where a spark is ignited. Go a step further and set up an apprenticeship or apply for a position when a passion emerges.

This advice has all been under the assumption that you have taken high school seriously. Maybe I should back up for those who are still in their teens. Try to understand and appreciate school for what it is: an opportunity to learn. Citizens, as taxpayers, supply large amounts of money to provide our youth with a solid educational foundation. The big picture can be hard to see at this point, but trust me, it does exist. Skipping school, ignoring homework, and prioritizing social affairs over academics is a recipe for disaster. Have fun, but not at the expense of sacrificing your professional future. Focus on improving those three familiar letters: GPA. Continue to demonstrate that same discipline in college, the next phase that will put you one step closer to landing your dream job. Along the way, keep in mind: There is no age requirement for being a difference maker. You are never too young to change the world.

Money Can't Buy Happiness

If you are a university alum fresh on the market, avoid the mistake of diving headfirst into an eight-to-five job solely based on income. Yes, financial stability is critical for you and your family, but don't let dollar signs hypnotize you into accepting a position you may later regret. A Christian brother of mine stepped down from his day job because he was "feeding the beast" that had a strong appetite for greed. The saying is true: Money can't buy happiness. Receive compensation for doing what you love. Before accepting a final offer, write out a pros and cons list. Include your loved ones so they can identify any red flags lying in the brush. Ask family and friends for input, weigh all your options, and confidently make the best decision.

Characteristics of a Good Employee

To many of you, your high school and college days are a distant memory. You may have been in the workforce so long, it's all you can remember. Have you made a valuable contribution to your company? Would others consider you a good employee? What constitutes a good employee? While there are many attributes to assess, here are a few of my favorites. Ask yourself if your colleagues would say you meet, or even exceed, these standards:

Accountability is a character trait employers will always value. It serves as a deep-rooted system that provides nutrients for other qualities to surface. We are hired with the intent that we can perform the work we are assigned. Can management and our colleagues count on us, day in and day out? Trust is an essential element for building a healthy working relationship with our peers. Establishing confidence among members within the organization allows them to perform their respective tasks more efficiently. The probability of accomplishing long-term success individually is slim to none, even if you transform into Superman upon walking through the front door. Any prosperous businessman or woman will tell you that teamwork really does make the dream work. Enjoy your role as a hard-working cog in the middle of a well-oiled machine. Lastly, punctuality most certainly fits in this category. Being on time and mentally prepared to tackle each work day is an integral part of that assumed responsibility. (Admittedly, Holly and I share a family history of tardiness: a condition we are desperately trying to outlive.)

Accountability may seem hollow if not paired with another highly sought-after characteristic: the right *attitude*. Do you convey passion in your work and infuse positivity into those around you? Show your passion by expending more energy than is required and going above and beyond. Can you break out of the mundane and give 100 percent to whatever task is handed to you? Whether you are assigned an A or C job, you should always bring your A game. Being extraordinary is when the ordinary add that little *extra*. Oftentimes, that little extra can manifest in the way you treat others. Show respect to all. Build your coworkers up by highlighting their strengths; don't tear them down by dwelling on their weaknesses. Always examine your intentions before voicing your displeasure. Are you looking for an avenue for improvement or an excuse to gossip? Ask yourself if you are blessing or blasting others.

We might not spring off the mattress every morning, leap in the car with excitement, and head straight to the office. And that's okay—no one is demanding that form of admiration toward our occupation. However, if we already make a physical appearance, why not bring the emotional aspect along for the ride? Show your boss, colleagues, and customers you are valuable. An outside observer can easily differentiate between those who put in an honest day's work and the minimalists who do just enough to get by. Perform with a purpose.

Another suggestion for digestion is to be aware of your nonverbal cues. Focus not only on *what* you say, but *how* you say it. Good eye contact, a firm handshake, appropriate dress attire (no, yoga pants don't qualify as business casual), facial expressions, hand gestures, posture, pep in your step, and tone of voice all synergistically matter. What would your body language say about your purpose? Can you be caught moving at a snail's pace and slouching over with your eyes fixed on the floor? You are likely broadcasting a silent message, one that you wouldn't ever approve of verbally divulging. *Undercover Boss* is a reality show that displays the true essence of working through clear glass and being visible to millions. Imagine your current opaque, secluded cubicle as an open, transparent exhibit, allowing spectators to view your every move. Work like everyone is always watching.

My Professional Journey

As previously explained, deciding on a career field is not easy for everyone. You may have your destination figured out from the beginning; enjoy that certainty. I, however, was not that fortunate. My journey commenced in the world of psychology. I became fascinated with the opportunity to improve the minds and, in turn, the lives of others. My desire to help others led me to a Bachelor of Arts in Psychology. However, upon completion of my degree, I decided to switch gears.

Back at the drawing board, I thought a profession in the medical world sounded interesting. I contemplated pre-med or nursing, but my uneasiness with blood and guts steered me in another direction. Still wanting to positively impact the health of those around me, while remaining a little less hands-on, the door to pharmacy opened. I waved good-bye to psychology classes of reading, lectures, and group discussions and said hello to science in the form of properties, calculations, and labs. To jump-start my career, I elected to enroll in a general chemistry summer course. I left my campus job in search of a firsthand experience in my new field.

Great fortune would have it that my answer lived one-third of a mile down the road. Our great friends and neighbors were a husband and wife duo, Dave and Evelyn, who owned and operated an independent pharmacy. Dave, the pharmacist-in-charge, was the friendly face in the white coat for many years, until a fatal auto accident at the speedway. (Dave, may God rest your soul as you sing with the angels.) Sadly, I wasn't able to witness him in his element behind the counter, but thankfully, Evelyn continued to manage the business and provided me the opportunity to get my feet wet when my interest in the profession arose.

I instantly loved the ability to positively impact lives and build relationships with the community. Throughout school, I explored a variety of settings and finally came across my saving grace: ambulatory care. This avenue unearthed a perfect fit: the one-on-one consulting of psychology in the midst of the medical realm. A couple job interviews later, I discovered the position I sought and received the call soon thereafter.

Did my professional preparation take a little bit? If you consider eight and a half years a little bit, then yes. Was it a bumpy road with unexpected twists and turns? Uh huh. Overall, was the ride worth the ebbs and flows I experienced? Most definitely. Are there still moments I want to pull my hair out? No doubt, but isn't that a universal feeling? I can tell you that every night my head hits the pillow, I am grateful for God leading me down the path He did. I give thanks for the ability to wake up loving my trade. I leave the house every morning mentally armed and dangerous, ready to make a difference.

I have enjoyed a steady blend of conventional retail and ambulatory care. Having a hand in people's accomplishments is the most rewarding aspect of my work. I live vicariously through our patients and find extreme happiness in the loss of fifty pounds, the A1C drop of 2 percent, the kick of a smoking habit, or the simplification of a medication regimen. Witnessing transformations in knowledge, confidence, and energy is inspirational music to my soul.

There's my vocational timeline laid out before you. Did you embark on a similar journey? Maybe you were always destined for your present occupation and received a calling early on. Perhaps you are still bumbling, stumbling, and fumbling in the dark. Either way, we all navigate different paths in life, so it's no surprise our professional voyages follow suit. Enjoy your journey, and appreciate your surroundings along the way. If you haven't found your perfect job—relax. Stay alert and open to opportunities that will arise before you; they are on their way.

Chapter 11

SHIFTING OUR FOCUS

*T*he world seems to be changing more and more every day, so what you aspire for today might be what you dread tomorrow. The spotlight is often cast on numbers of clients, daily sales, and profit. While these are solid goals for a company, can we please not forget or lose sight of loyalty, sympathy, and respect? Corporate America is busy writing checks employees can't cash. Granted, I'm not a CEO, nor do I routinely view the entire forest from a helicopter perspective. It's plausible I would share a different sentiment if I held a higher position on the ladder, although I honestly hope not. I can tell you from my vantage point, it's getting kind of lonely down here among the trees. It is incredibly hard for me to witness compassion being replaced by greed. The endless demands of proprietors have resulted in an overabundant supply of cutthroat, productivity-centered environments and a dire shortage of basic humanity.

I realize we are all sinful and selfish creatures by nature—myself included. Not one of us has earned the right to cast the first stone. I propose an urgent meeting where we go back to the drawing board and allow ourselves an opportunity for improvement. The first step in Problem Solving 101 is admitting you have a problem; we have a problem. We can all likely find ourselves in one of these following areas; I know I can. I'm optimistic that exposing and addressing some of our weaknesses will ultimately help us reach a solution.

Overcome with Selfishness

(Gavel in hand) Let's get started by being honest with ourselves. We currently live in a "me" driven society and are quick to satisfy our own needs and wants. Many of us work long hours, feeding whatever beast is consuming us. We mistakenly try to achieve fulfillment through means of materialistic equity: a bigger house, newer car, or designer wardrobe. We often hold on to the phrase, "If only I had _____, my life would be complete." If money is the goal, we will never have enough. This happiness-buying mentality only clouds our judgment, leaves us feeling empty, and sets us up for prolonged failure. We, as Americans, have been so accurately described as rich in materials but poor in spirit.

Enthroned by Entitlement

Entitlement is ever prominent in our world today. We hear the phrase, "Work smarter, not harder." We live with "snap our fingers" expectations. Many of us in today's generation aren't willing to get our hands dirty, nor do we know the meaning of hard labor. We are lazy, and that's not okay. We've listened to our parents and grandparents begin their stories with, "Well, when I was your age, we had to …" We can't see any correlation between our elders' stories of suffering and our effortless ability to navigate life. In our eyes, that was them back then, and this is us right now.

Consumed by Technology

The progression of technology certainly carries advantages, but it comes at the cost of regression in authenticity toward our brothers and sisters in Christ. We mindlessly scroll on newsfeeds, eagerly waiting for the next big event to be reported. Cell phones, computers, and other gadgets have become a crutch to avoid real conversation. We can text ninety miles a minute but can't hold eye contact for more than a few seconds. I'm pleading that we put down our phones and look up. The world is not inside our electronics; the world is around us, and we are missing it.

Deprived of Purpose

There seems to be a fundamental flaw in today's society: An abundance of professions are void of passion. Many of us work simply to earn a paycheck and put food on the table. I'm certainly not discrediting financial independence, but I believe there are far too many people settling in their vocations today. We are unknowingly painting a picture in our children's heads that our eight-to-five is just something we *have* to do every day. What about their eight-to-five—school? Have we unintentionally taught our little ones to dread class and homework assignments? Don't we know these obligations are monumentally important for their futures? If we aren't careful, we are going to convince kids that vocation, along with education, is a forced and unpleasant activity. How quickly we forget that citizens of underdeveloped nations aren't offered these privileges we so often take for granted.

Our One and Only Solution

Let's face it: We are lost at sea and subconsciously taking on water in the wake of a storm of gigantic proportions. How do we right the ship? Perhaps we should look at a more practical application. Where do we as consumers look for answers when a product is faulty, the assembly proves challenging, or we want to operate more efficiently? The most reliable source I've found is the owner's manual. After all, the manufacturer has the greatest expertise. Why wouldn't the same principle hold true for navigating life, including our vocation? Doesn't it make sense that we should seek counsel from the One Who created us?

I wholeheartedly believe God has a unique mission for every single one of His sons and daughters. It's up to each one of us to develop a relationship with our Creator and find our purpose. Just as we grow in our relationships with others, we must invest the necessary time to deepen that bond with our Father. Striving each day to become closer to our Maker and discovering His intentions for us are both the beauty and adventure of life. When we individually discipline ourselves to make that a reality, we become part of the solution to all of our problems.

From Selfishness to Sacrifice

While spending time in daily prayer, our self-seeking behavior will start to fade. We will realize that our past desires were likely for wants, not needs. Besides, too much house lends itself to too much space between family members. Learn from the biblical wisdom of Solomon in the book of Ecclesiastes: A life of excess is meaningless and only leads to a deeper void in the heart. Instead of trying to keep up with the Joneses, we need to try to keep up with Jesus. When we are introduced to God's true nature, His sacrificial ways will rub off on us, and our primary objective will shift from receiving to giving.

From Entitlement to Gratitude

While spending time in daily prayer, our feelings of entitlement will turn to gratitude. While we may still strive to work smarter, not harder, we won't complain about working hard when necessary. The long-winded tales of suffering from our elders that once made us impatient will leave us feeling extremely grateful and appreciative of their character. We will do all we can to sustain that zealous work ethic of our bloodline.

From Emojis to Emotions

While spending time in daily prayer, we will see how priceless relationships are. Rather than using people and loving things, we will use things and love people. We may still enjoy the benefits of technology, but we won't let them consume us. We will see that attention on social media is nothing compared to a genuine, heartfelt, face-to-face interaction. While still cherishing the ability to communicate with those far away, we will put more emphasis on spending quality time with those we are fortunate to have near.

From Settling to Thriving

If you haven't found any advice to chew on, here's the whole enchilada: While spending time in daily prayer, you will uncover your passion and true vocation. In the olden days, people used to barter, without money, based on their mastered skill. We are all born with different strengths and have access to difference resources. God's brilliant design created us in a unique manner. We aren't robotic drones or monkeys who march to the beat of the same drum. What may bore one will energize another. While some are infused with creativity to burn, others excel with a step-by-step plan. Are you a creature of habit who prefers routine? Or are you a lover of surprises waiting around the next corner?

Without a sense of our strengths, weaknesses, and personality type, we can become lost. My first cut as a surgeon would leave me as flat on the floor as the patient. Don't confuse me for a tour guide; I get lost in the bathtub. Forget filling a seat at my concert, because of the 270 bones I was born with, not a single one is musical. However, when people start talking about wanting to improve their health, I'm all in.

With God in your heart, your strengths will come into focus. You will be proactive, not reactive. Initiative is untouchable. Work will have a whole new meaning. You will thrive in your abilities in addition to simply earning a paycheck. You will come to understand and appreciate the impact you can make on your community, and you will be excited about the opportunity to go to work every day and make a difference. You will change your attitude and show young, impressionable minds what you *get* to do for a living. You will live with an insatiable thirst to fulfill your purpose.

As an example of someone who has found his purpose, I introduce to you Dick Vitale, more commonly known as Dicky V. This college basketball sportscaster who adamantly professes his love for the game is the epitome of passion. Dicky V regularly tries to comprehend how he can be paid to do something he loves so much; he believes he's been stealing cash all these years because of the fun he's having. Vitale is seventy-eight, going on five. He credits finding passion through his faith, family, and core values. When your occupation fills you with as much sheer joy as Dicky V's announcing does for him, congratulations—you have made it, my friend.

On a more personal level, I have witnessed vocational excellence firsthand from my favorite college professor. Tysha had me ready to set this world on fire after sitting through her first class. She has been such a powerful source of inspiration for me ever since, as I will forever treasure the priceless gems she entrusted to us.

While Tysha ignited my spark, Pastor Mark Hoover of NewSpring Church continually fans the flame. God uses this amazing servant of a man as His instrument to orchestrate a masterpiece every service. His son and associate pastor, Jonathan, is following in his dad's footsteps; he does an incredible job in his own right. Their words have truly changed my life. I am beyond grateful for their blessing to share their undeniably God-inspired wisdom throughout this book. The passion that exudes from their captivating messages (along with the spirit-filled anthems from the praise and worship team) fiercely invigorates my soul to spread the love of Jesus each week. I encourage you to search high and low to unearth an intensity that will emanate through you and spread to others. John Wesley said it best: "Catch on fire with enthusiasm and people will come for miles to watch you burn."

The Art of Compartmentalizing

Regardless of our level of passion for our profession, stress is inevitable. Remember that those eight hours (or more) on the job can shape the remainder of the day. Some are fortunate enough to effortlessly leave their stress at the office. However, many of us allow worries to linger, weigh heavily, and consequently affect our home life. (Do you remember transference from chapter 5?) The ability to compartmentalize work and home is monumental toward maintaining healthy relationships and improving mental well-being. As we have learned, our *quantity* of time with loved ones is already less than what we wish it to be; don't hinder the *quality* as well.

Accepting the Challenge

In your constant journey to find purpose, continue studying His owner's manual: the Bible. God has a promising, albeit mysterious, plan. Although we don't share His level of intelligence to understand each step, we must trust in His brilliant design. Admittedly, biblical teachings are full of complexity, but allow me to provide a couple of take-home and take-to-work points, which happen to be Jesus' two greatest commandments, according to Matthew 22:

- "You must love the Lord your God with all your heart, all your soul, and all your mind" (v. 37).
- "Love your neighbor as yourself" (v. 39).

If you aren't currently living according to these principles, I challenge you to make God your first priority. You will be amazed by how the transformation will carry over into your vocation and everyday life. Where you might have previously asked, "What can you do for me?" you will be enlightened to offer, "What can I do for you?" And remember that perfection doesn't exist, but happiness surely does. When we love what we are doing, it's visible for others to see, and our happiness becomes contagious. As *Unspoken* sings, "You only need a spark to start a whole blaze." (We know from chapter 5 that anger can quickly spread; that same philosophy holds true for positivity.) When you trust in and invest in God, the fruition of true happiness will seemingly unfold in your lap.

Finally, I lay these challenges before you: Pursue a vocation that enables you to use your God-given talent. Incorporate passion in the *perfect* job God has placed on your heart to fulfill. Act as His hands and feet to make a difference for others every single day.

Consider these lasting tips when searching for or re-evaluating your vocation:

- Take initiative.
- Embrace change.

- Work with a purpose.
- Invite lifelong learning.
- Seek out a good mentor.
- Practice and perfect your craft.
- Formulate a pros and cons list for decision-making.
- Find something you love to do, and you will never work a day in your life.
- Make your work, no matter how small, a form of worship for the Lord.

(We all have the same employer, and He's always watching.)

Chapter 12

FROM THE LIVING WORD: NEHEMIAH'S UNWAVERING DETERMINATION

 We meet our next biblical character, Nehemiah, midway through the Old Testament. He narrates his own story as a prisoner exiled from Jerusalem to the foreign land of Babylon, which was later overtaken by Persia. Years into his captivity, he became the royal cupbearer to King Artaxerxes, a position of high standing in the Persian court. Upon receiving devastating news from a fellow Israelite that their homeland was in ruins and the survivors were in grave trouble, Nehemiah demonstrated an immediate sign of homage to his town, people, and almighty Savior. It wasn't a robotic, half-hearted, "Oh no. That's too bad, but I've got a pretty good thing going here," kind of response. Nehemiah was deeply moved to tears. Then, he mourned, fasted, and prayed, not for minutes or hours, but rather days.

We see Nehemiah's faith come front and center when he pleads to God. Before any consideration of heavenly intervention, Nehemiah's first order of business was a confession of sin for himself, his family, and the entire Israelite community. Notice that he never shook his fist or demanded an explanation for God's wrath, nor did he shed the blame. Instead, he admitted fault for all the corruption and accepted punishment. Being a student of Mosaic law, Nehemiah reminded

God of the redeeming power of His mercy and grace to those who earnestly repent.

Nehemiah was still brokenhearted while later serving wine to King Artaxerxes. With a heavenly push, he asked to return home to rebuild the wall of Jerusalem and even requested materials for construction, as well as protection throughout his journey. Coming from a servant who had no ground to stand on, these were brave requests to a foreign king. To the secular mind, this was a lunatic digging his own grave. Ah, but we forget it was God Himself Who put this objective in Nehemiah's heart.

Upon his homecoming and attempt at restoration, Nehemiah's initial covert mission was to inspect the wall in the secrecy of the night. After surveying the land, he boldly approached the Jewish priests, nobles, and officials to reveal the master plan. He assured them God's hand was at work and that he had the king of Persia's approval. They were all in.

However, Nehemiah and his men were met with immediate resistance once the word spread. Nearby officials ridiculed the Israelites for undertaking such an enormous task and mocked the strength of their materials. Nehemiah continually turned the other cheek and offered his hardships up to God. When his adversaries learned of their swift progress, they became furious and made plans to attack Jerusalem. Once again, Nehemiah relied on God's strength.

Negativity spread throughout the minds of his own men, who complained of wearing down from moving all the rubble. Again, their enemies made threats of physical violence, and his people became fearful. Nehemiah responded by stationing half his men as guards to protect vulnerable areas. Most importantly, he reminded them to be steadfast in their faith because the Lord was with them. Nehemiah rallied the troops, and in the face of danger, he infused them with courage.

When outside officials realized the rebuilding was near completion, they attempted to halt production by summoning Nehemiah for meetings in neighboring villages. Nehemiah knew these requests were only a ploy to cause harm; he kept his eye on the prize of finishing the wall and labored with even more determination. When Nehemiah declined a fourth invitation, his enemies initiated a rumor of his intentions to revolt against the king. He responded by simply praying for the Lord to strengthen his hands.

Another wave of conflict presented itself: a foe disguised as friend. After conspiring with adversaries, a fellow Israelite shared a false prophesy so Nehemiah would run and hide. Full of God-given wisdom, Nehemiah recognized that the evil scheme was brought about to cause intimidation, isolate him, and discredit his honor in front of his people.

Adding to the laundry list of challenges was the discovery that Jerusalem's officials were being unfair to their own people. Hearing the outcry of the oppressed, our mighty warrior gathered the community to address the situation. He courageously scolded the officials for punishing through high taxes, withholding food, and subjecting children to slavery in the midst of the famine. Furthermore, Nehemiah amended the suffering and established an oath stating this unjust behavior would not be repeated. He also decided to forgo his entitled rights as a governor, after witnessing others' burdens. Imitating the selfless nature of Jesus, Nehemiah publically demonstrated he wasn't any more significant than the least of his people.

Despite numerous attempts from several different sources to prevent the rebuilding of the wall, Nehemiah and his people finished in an astonishing fifty-two days. Neighboring lands trembled with fear when they caught word of the miraculous feat, knowing the work had been guided by Israel's God. Rebuilding the wall was Nehemiah's first step, but his ultimate quest was to re-establish the Israelite family under the grace of God. He recovered a genealogical record, brought his people out of captivity, and restored the city. He appointed leaders of high integrity to govern the city. With Ezra the Priest, he planned a celebration to dedicate the wall and renew the covenant of Moses.

Nehemiah had righted the ship; therefore, he departed for Persia and resumed his place in the king's court. When he returned to

Jerusalem years later, he observed many wrongdoings. He quickly scolded, corrected, and purified the city once again. The chapter of Nehemiah is bookended in the same manner it began, as we find our hero deep in prayer.

We can learn a great deal from Nehemiah's work ethic and overall character. He experienced abuse, deception, discontent, intimidation, guilt—you name it. With the multitude of body blows, both physical and emotional, and the incessant attempts of defamation toward Nehemiah, it is astounding there wasn't even an ounce of backlash. Can you imagine the emotional load he endured? At times, he must have felt like the proverbial walls were caving in on him.

We all experience our fair share of opposition, but unlike Nehemiah, our first reaction is often to seek revenge. With physical aggression unquestionably prohibited at the workplace, we counter with word of mouth and usually end up leaving more lasting scars than a black eye or bloody lip. Up against the ropes, we frequently resort to participating in tempting, juicy gossip around the water cooler (or wherever the guilty parties congregate). First lady Eleanor Roosevelt wisely stated: "Great minds discuss ideas; average minds discuss events; small minds discuss people."

Injecting a little truth serum, I'm forced to admit I'm not always an innocent bystander. However, the enormous amount of ensuing guilt proves to be a powerful reminder of my wicked tongue and leaves me shaking my head every single time. The strategy of belittling others in order to gain self-confidence is flawed on so many levels. Satan willingly gives us a false sense of happiness, disguised as pleasure, because we initially feel better. Comparing our shortcomings to others', which the Bible clearly instructs us not to do, allows us to rationally minimize our faults and shed any blame or wrongdoing on our end. We will never be truly fulfilled if humiliating others is our go-to method to elevate our self-esteem. However, those who love and pray for their enemies have a promised seat in heaven that nothing in this world can ever compete with. When you find yourself immersed in daily drama, ignore the temporary verbal trash *around* you and focus on His eternally vowed treasure *above* you.

Apart from relationships, how do we handle the adversity of our day-to-day workload? Do we regularly pray for God's guidance at work when times are tough? Too often, we stumble upon obstacles, and when a challenge arises and proves to be too difficult (in our estimation), we prematurely throw in the towel. During these make-or-break moments, Satan knows full well our potential and what lies ahead should we succeed. He is quick to deceive, regularly convincing us that ordinary roadblocks or detours are actually stop signs. When we give up, Satan wins; when he wins, we always lose.

You and I face—and will continue to face—many storms in our lives every day. Though not always favorable, God's plan will never lead you to a storm that His grace won't help you overcome. During each hardship, Nehemiah let go of his anxieties and looked to heaven; when fear came knocking, he let faith answer.

Without knowledge of Nehemiah's faith, we could easily lose hope for our beloved character after reading his parade of trials and tribulations. Yet throughout his labor, Nehemiah never let anyone or anything stand in the way of his mission of rebuilding the wall. Romans 8:31 reminds us, "If God is for us, who can ever be against us?" We must learn (and, more importantly, apply) this monumental lesson of dependence on and trust in God. The next time you encounter what seem like insurmountable odds, listen to the lyrics (adapted a bit) from Love & The Outcome: "Throw your hands up and your worries down." Keep fighting, pursue your mission, and overcome Satan's barriers; your treasure awaits you.

How many of us envision a chest full of gold when we see the word "treasure"? We will be sadly mistaken if that's the prize we are seeking. Earthly riches have Satan's greedy fingerprints all over them. Nehemiah had access to wealth but chose not to partake in his rightly earned indulgences when he observed that the less fortunate were barely surviving. Could you happily give up your luxuries of fine wining and dining? Could you forfeit your end-of-the-year bonus and distribute the money evenly among your employees? Could you offer up your private, corner office with a view? Could you give it all up, knowing you were pleasing God?

I'd like to share some lasting remarks from Dr. Kent M. Keith, who provides us encouragement for when we are faced with adversity.

The Paradoxical Commandments
by Dr. Kent M. Keith

People are illogical, unreasonable, and self-centered.
Love them anyway.

If you do good, people will accuse you of selfish ulterior motives.
Do good anyway.

If you are successful, you will win false friends and true enemies.
Succeed anyway.

The good you do today will be forgotten tomorrow.
Do good anyway.

Honesty and frankness make you vulnerable.
Be honest and frank anyway.

The biggest men and women with the biggest ideas can be shot down by the smallest men and women with the smallest minds.
Think big anyway.

People favor underdogs but follow only top dogs.
Fight for a few underdogs anyway.

What you spend years building may be destroyed overnight.
Build anyway.

People really need help but may attack you if you do help them.
Help people anyway.

Give the world the best you have and you'll get kicked in the teeth.
Give the world the best you have anyway.

Dr. Keith captured the beauty of sacrifice, forgiveness, and love with this gem that reminds us to remain compliant with God's will, even without positive feedback. You will likely be disappointed if you wait for those you bless to return the favor. However, when you willingly continue to offer unconditional love, you will receive God's blessing, and there is no greater honor.

Part 4

FOURTH PUZZLE EDGE: FAITH

Faith: *Confident belief in the truth, value, or trustworthiness of a person, idea, or thing.*
—The American Heritage College Dictionary

Faith shows the reality of what we hope for; it is the evidence of things we cannot see.
—Hebrews 11:1

Chapter 13

OUR JOURNEY THROUGH FAITH

*S*uppose we had boxes to check yes or no for the questions: Is parenting crucial? Do relationships matter? Are jobs important? I would like to think we could come to a consensus with a resounding yes. Without parents, we wouldn't have anyone to show us the way of life. Starved of friends and family, we wouldn't have anyone to share in life's experiences. Take away income, and we wouldn't be able to provide for ourselves or our families. Those rationalizations all seem like no-brainers, but if we consider the proposal, "Is faith essential?", our affirmations might not be so unanimous. However, I sincerely hope that we can also willingly attach a yes to this query by the end of our discussion.

Faith is the core of my existence, yet I know not everyone embodies the same belief. Therefore, please treat these next few chapters as an open invitation to make a personal choice, not an unwarranted smothering or brainwashing session. After a self-inflicted interrogation of my heart, I realized I ultimately desire the wisdom to inspire and encourage each of my readers to accept Christ; I pray He uses my words to personally reach each and every one of you. In my ambitious nature, my hope is that we can all collectively spread His message of love and help lead as many souls to heaven as possible.

With that being said, let's unassumingly step out of our comfy shoes, open up our consciences, leave the tunnel vision behind, strip ourselves of the judging glasses, and explore like never before. Throwing a blanket statement of disagreement over everything you don't believe in or fully understand is the easy way out. I am wholeheartedly pleading that you keep your rebuttal at bay—at least initially. In return, I will do my absolute best to meet you where you are and not be too preachy, in fear of losing your interest. (Although I must disclose, I am the grandson of a devoted preacher.) If our discussion doesn't alter your lenses, feel free to sink back into your slippers and re-enter your comfort zone; we can continue to respectfully agree to disagree.

Without further ado, let's journey together. You can anticipate a few stops along the way. First, we will be taking faith at face value from a couple of outsiders' perspectives, followed by my folk, who deem it indispensable, and finally from the throne of God. Remember the rules: no finger-pointing, head-shaking, or anything defensive by nature. Got it? Good. Here we go …

Perspective One: Why Do I Need God?

Now this beginning stance, I confess, is emotionally arduous for me. Nonetheless, I will take a stab at it for the sake of this mental exercise. I have a good friend who represents this view, so I will do my best to summarize what I have gathered through some of our deeper conversations.

> From his standpoint: Why do I need faith? I delight in my lovely wife, three beautiful children, and a promising career that allows me to provide for my family. I would like to think my achievements are a result of my own doing. I am proud of the fact I don't require assistance from others. I treat people the right way and expect to be treated in a similar fashion. There are things I cannot explain, and rather than simply assimilate, I choose to use logic and reasoning in my understanding. That's not to say I will always hold this position, but with my inability to blindly

believe, anything but a life-changing moment will likely leave me short of conversion.

I recently put this "holy God" to the ultimate test. After conducting my own research through literary works and much dialogue, I finally put myself out there. One night while the rest of my family was asleep, I anxiously headed outside to an open field and knelt down to offer this prayer: "Okay God, here I am. The masses have recommended you. I grew up with you in the household, but after many years, I haven't seen a need to continue our relationship. Now, after much discernment, I choose to give it another try. If you are real, my only wish is for you to send me an unmistakable sign, just so I know you are listening and really do care about me." I waited for ten minutes, with my eyes laser-focused, heart inviting, and arms wide open—but to no avail. Arising from my knees with a nasty taste of rejection, I slumped back inside and slid into bed. My skepticism remains to this day. That night of disappointment hasn't led me to completely close the book on Christianity, but I am still waiting on a significant flash of heavenly origin to push me over the edge.

There are voluminous realities I tussle with on a daily basis. How can a precious, innocent seven-year-old be savagely consumed by an incurable form of brain cancer? Why do tornadoes, hurricanes, and earthquakes unapologetically slay thousands every year? What explainable justice can we attribute for horrendous acts such as abuse, rape, and murder? Why is heaven not a reward earned on our own merits? If I treat people the right way, shouldn't that be enough to receive heaven? Wouldn't a loving God observe my big heart? After surveying the field, I honestly feel I am in better standing than many Christians today.

How does it make sense they should enter the pearly
gates instead of me?

My friend brings up so many good points, and some I can't
answer. I suppose he lives with the mentality, "If it's not broke, don't
fix it." His life is full of favor. His contentment has given him no
reason to change his lifestyle. He rests on the thought that things
will all sort themselves out if he continues to live as a good person.

Why Does God Let Bad Things Happen?

Boy, if I had a nickel for every time this question comes up, I'd be rich.
Allow me to offer a twofold explanation to put this debate to rest: our
ultimate, universal enemy and free will. The words of 1 Peter 5:8–9
afford me ammunition to help explain the former: "Stay alert! Watch
out for your great enemy, the devil. He prowls around like a roaring
lion, looking for someone to devour. Stand firm against him, and be
strong in your faith. Remember that your family of believers all over
the world is going through the same kind of suffering you are." Please
keep in mind that Satan revels as an influential presence in our daily
lives. Temptation is always at our fingertips, and in our weaknesses,
we repeatedly succumb to his prodding and carry out our sinful ways.

Free will allows for poor decision-making that leads to unfavorable
consequences, but it also saves us from being the mere by-products of
robotic hardwiring. Thankfully, we aren't dancing puppets; rather,
we are wonderfully and fearfully made, with a sense of personal
uniqueness and intellect. This earth is full of hardships and obvious
tragedy. There's no denying this reality. Natural disasters are difficult
to justify, although they are just that: *natural*. They are part of the
flawed world we live in. We certainly aren't perfect, so why should
we expect that of our habitat?

How do I rationalize a precious, innocent seven-year-old savagely
consumed by an incurable form of brain cancer? I simply cannot.
Along with catastrophic events, freak accidents, sudden losses, and
many other causes of heartbreak, I honestly don't think any amount

of deliberation can help us fully understand the reasoning. And I don't think it's productive to try. As Isaiah 55:8–9 reads, "'My thoughts are nothing like your thoughts,' says the Lord. 'And my ways are far beyond anything you could imagine. For just as the heavens are higher than the earth, so my ways are higher than your ways and my thoughts higher than your thoughts.'" Think of children's innocence to nutrition as an example we can grasp. Kids don't see anything wrong with eating sugar all day, every day. Parents know the detriments of consuming excess amounts, as well as the benefits of eating a well-balanced diet. To youngers, limiting sugar-laden foods might seem inconsiderate and downright mean. After all, why would you want to take away something so delicious and deprive them of pleasure? It's simple, because you understand the big picture and how it affects their health, and they don't. In a similar manner, our brains weren't designed with the capacity to make sense of everything around us, and it's hard for me to doubt the One Who is omnipotent (all-powerful), omnipresent (all-present), and omniscient (all-knowing). The Pollyanna in me says this: The self-inflicted wickedness of society and the destruction by Mother Nature provide us with purpose and ample opportunities to show our true colors of humanity toward one another. And we often do; the responses to Hurricane Katrina and 9/11, along with numerous other circumstances, unified our nation. Here's where I find my ultimate rest: faith in a heaven that promises freedom from injury, illness, suffering, and pain. No matter how hard he tries, Satan has no pull once we arrive in God's imperishable kingdom.

Is Being *Good* Enough?

Discerning qualifications for where someone spends eternity is far beyond my credentials, so I rely on scripture. The Bible is explicit on how one gets to heaven: a belief in and a relationship with Christ. Honestly, I really struggle with making sense of the pathway to the pearly gates. This may be a better topic for your local pastor, but here's my best explanation: Our brains can't process the amazing, breathtaking perfection of heaven. Because of this limitation, we often deny its existence or downplay its significance. Some even assume the role of gatekeeper and feel that entry to heaven should be performance-based and reserved solely for good people who say and do the right things.

Herein lies the problem: We will never *earn* our way past the gates. And comparison with or judgment toward another certainly doesn't give us an edge or make us any more worthy. As Matthew 7:3-4 points out, "Why worry about a speck in your friend's eye when you have a log in your own? How can you think of saying to your friend, 'Let me help you get rid of that speck in your eye,' when you can't see past the log in your own eye?" We are all sinful people and fall short of entering heaven without intervention from above.

This life tells us that we can have anything we want if we work hard enough. Heaven is different. We can't buy, volunteer, study, pray, or even sacrifice our way in. We can exhaust all our options, but to no avail, and here's why: The price for our salvation is the sacrifice of a perfect son. Does anyone have one? Sorry, Lucas; Daddy loves you, but you are far from perfect. We all are. The only father who meets the criteria is God. Therefore, the price for our salvation is ... nothing but the blood of Jesus.

Jesus is the perfect Son, Who willingly offered up His life when He was crucified on a cross. According to John 19:30, He muttered, "*It* is finished!" moments before He breathed His last. That *it* was the price being paid. It will never be about what we do; it has always been and always will be about what *He* did—for us. He has done the hard part. Our sole requirements are to acknowledge His existence, accept His free gift, and RSVP to His table.

Let's quickly dispel a common myth: God doesn't deny anyone heaven; they simply choose not to accept His invitation. Matthew 10:32–33 states, "Everyone who acknowledges me publicly here on earth, I will also acknowledge before my Father in heaven. But everyone who denies me here on earth, I will also deny before my Father in heaven." We serve a loving God Who doesn't demand redemption; He waits patiently with open arms—not forceful hands.

Movie Lifeline

If you haven't seen *God's Not Dead,* rent this gem for your next movie night. Actor Dean Cain (better known as Superman) lives by the same logic my friend holds. His character, Marc Shelley, is a nonbeliever who doesn't feel the need for a divine relationship. From the outside, he appears to have it all: a prestigious career, a beautiful woman, and the world at his fingertips. However, he struggles to believe in a higher power who would allow his mother, a devout Christian, to mentally wither away from dementia. In one particular scene, he desperately searches for rationale, becoming frustrated by the cognitive dissonance between the presence of faith and the corresponding level of suffering in their respective lives. We listen as he rambles on to his mother about fairness, not anticipating a response in her current mental state of confusion. Her screen time up to this point has been nothing short of a movie extra. Viewers are likely feeling deeply saddened (like I was) for a helpless and mute woman, who in her disorientation displays only wandering eyes and an empty soul. That pity quickly changes, so make sure your popcorn bowl is full and your bladder is empty. What a powerful moment of cinema. Pay close attention as the monologue becomes an unexpected conversation Marc, and now we, will never forget.

Whatever it was in her that seemed lost is instantly found. Before our eyes, she transforms into a messenger more powerful and better equipped than Superman. She hits us at the core when she unleashes the Holy Spirit dwelling inside her and begins to preach these words from deep in her heart: "Sometimes the devil allows people to live a life free of trouble 'cause he doesn't want them turning to God. Your sin is like a jail cell, except it's all nice and comfy, and there doesn't seem to be any need to leave. The door's wide open until one day time runs out, the cell door slams shut, and suddenly it's too late." Then, just as quickly as she passionately came to life, her lights go dim, and she slips back into oblivion, unable to identify her son once again.

The same anguish this mother expresses for her son's permanent destiny, I share for my friend. He enjoys a comfortable life that bears no reason to lean on anyone. He says, "I'm going to continue living life the best way I know how, with an overriding mission of serving others and leaving society better than I found it. If there is a god I want to be associated with, this way of life will be appreciated, and the doors to a personal relationship will be opened."

My friend's cumulative thoughts, words, and actions could be the measuring stick for good morale. And I wholeheartedly agree with him that his good works are more impressive than many Christians' today. Truth be told, if we all laid our cards on the table and achieved deliverance through our own works, he may be one of the first in line. His head is in the right place, but he has the wrong person sitting on the throne of his heart.

The journey of my friend's faith constantly challenges yet encourages me. Despite the secular perspective he holds onto, his lifestyle is hard to condemn; his compassion is always on display. He is one of the most caring human beings I know and remains a great friend of mine. In fact, upon the arrival of our firstborn, he made a surprise visit to the hospital from several hours away. Selflessness is engrained in him, and he knows no other way; that's what he feels is right. In seeing his genuine nature firsthand on multiple accounts, I immediately credit our heavenly Father. I rationalize that because God is the source of all good, and I witness the goodness my friend so commonly demonstrates, the Lord is undoubtedly present in his heart. (If a = b and b = c, then a = c.)

Thinking Outside the Box

Suppose you take the initiative to clean up a small park near your house, knowing this is a favorite hangout for the local community. One Saturday, you labor from sunup to sundown, feeling accomplished as you fall fast asleep later that night. The next morning, you wake to a crowd of neighbors chattering about the transformation, mistakenly giving credit to your next-door neighbor. Maybe we should stop right there and put ourselves in the moment. Would you be quick to fling the front door open, correct their false information, and accept your rightly earned praise? Or are you part of the minority who would be able to hold your tongue, calmly go about your day, and leave someone else with the glory?

My soul-searching friend would comfortably fall in the latter category. He would merely be content that the kids' playground was up to snuff and move on to another random act of kindness. Giving up recognition for the good deed in this hypothetical situation is simple for him, yet he remains prideful when claiming the credit for his benevolent motives. He is one step away from understanding that our heavenly Father is the perpetual source of virtue.

My friend is also one of the most intelligent individuals I know; he reads *Harvard Business Review*, for crying out loud. So, if reaching heaven was by way of an aptitude test, he would again be near the front. I thank God it's not, for my sake. As a result of his brilliant psyche, he yearns for logic and reasoning to prove the same faith that my soul blindly finds rest in. We share similar interests and seem quite alike in many ways (so much that my wife has repeatedly mistaken us for each other from behind), but there is one major divide: He lives for this life, and I live for the one to come.

Chapter 14

WHERE IS GOD IN ALL THIS?

$\mathcal{T}$he devil devises an array of clever schemes to distract us from receiving the Bread of Life. Frequently, the enemy entices us with delectable temptations and endless appeal. Sometimes, he satisfies our cravings through the comfort food of ordinary life, giving us little reason for a desire to alter our palate—like in my friend's case. Other times, he leaves us starving for a morsel of hope, as you will notice from the ensuing vantage point of another friend:

Perspective Two: Given Up on God

> Early into adulthood, I began suffering from chronic back pain. I elected to have surgery with the intent to relieve the discomfort and prevent further issues. However, the operation wasn't as successful as planned, and to alleviate my constant agony, I began using prescription medication. It wasn't long before I became not only dependent on, but addicted to, painkillers. They eventually became my gateway to recreational drugs, and I slowly started to lose touch with reality.
>
> Before I realized the consequences of my actions, I was riding a slippery slope and found it harder and harder to gain any traction. To make matters worse,

my husband was my partner in crime, and we isolated ourselves from family, friends, and the rest of the world. Normalcy no longer existed. I didn't know how to function without my crutch, and I lost all confidence in myself. Medication was my escape, and the resulting euphoric feeling was the only place where I felt peace. Eventually the euphoria dissipated, and I was left self-medicating to suppress all my mental and emotional pain. The agony of withdrawal was quick to remind me that I was enchained. My feelings were numb, my actions were uncharacteristic, and my priorities were skewed. Responsibility, love, and honesty were replaced with stealing, cheating, and lying.

In the midst of all the chaos, I found myself unexpectedly pregnant. This little girl was literally my life saver, as she is the reason I am now drug-free and working to get my life back in order. Each day is a battle of its own. My husband and I separated after battling issues of infidelity, control, and trust. We are still trying to figure out if we can happily live together for our daughter's sake. As far as my faith goes, I am no longer a believer. I don't see how a loving God could sit back and watch me endure so much suffering over all these years. What's more, I don't see why I should praise a higher power who could allow all this suffering in the world, especially to innocent children. It's not that I won't ever believe, I just need to see there is something worth believing in. My family keeps encouraging me to get back to church and give God a second chance. I have rekindled my relationships with them, but I'm not ready to forgive Him yet and may never be.

In recapping her account, she has no doubt encountered immeasurable dark and haunting days. From a spiritual standpoint, she has felt abandoned for quite some time. She owns the mind-set, "Why should I worship a so-called *god* who would let all those bad things happen to me?" Maybe you can't identify with this sense of betrayal. Do you know someone who can? If you are on top of the world right now, keep basking in the sunlight, but please remember to reach down and share your warmth with a soul in need today.

Offering Comfort

My counsel to her also applies to many of you idling through a dry season. My first response is always the caring embrace of a hug. In hearing and seeing the positive feedback over the years from this simple, yet powerful gesture, I am fueled with more than enough reason to continue. I believe this physical contact offers tangible sympathy; holding onto someone gives you assurance that you are not alone. Now that you know you have a friend in me, let's talk.

I won't pretend to know exactly how you feel; I certainly don't. However, I want you to know I'm truly sorry. I'm sorry you are in chronic pain, I'm sorry you are having conflict in your marriage, and I'm sorry for your overall unhappiness and discontentment with life. Most of all, I'm sorry you have given up on God. Of all the wrong turns or mistakes you think you have made up to this point, I believe turning your back on Him was the most costly. Please allow me to help you consider rekindling that relationship.

I am aware this reconciliation isn't a single-session, thirty-minute fix, but that shouldn't keep us from taking that necessary first step. Thank you in advance; rehashing your worst days probably won't be easy. I want you to unlock your file cabinet of memories and hunt for the folder labeled "Gave up on God." Sift through and revisit the details: What, when, where, why, and how? I recognize this could be too demanding of a request. Maybe your falling out wasn't a single affair but rather a gradual slide or chain of events. Keep thinking while I turn on the radio …

There are many instruments through which God speaks to me; music is one of the most powerful. Hillsong United's song "Oceans" always stops me dead in my tracks and reminds me of God's steadfast love. When we are in dire straits and searching for strength, believers needn't search any farther than songs from the *God's Not Dead* movies: "God's Not Dead" and "Guilty" by the Newsboys. However, I am fully aware that these God-filled anthems may not move mountains for agnostics, atheists, or uneasy souls. So let's browse **K-LOVE** radio's musical library to meet you where you are. The songs on this incredible station (along with other Christian radio stations) can provide you with answers to many of life's questions in the form of inspiration, courage, motivation, comfort, forgiveness, strength, hope, or love. For the sake of simplicity, I will hone in on a couple: "Worn" by Tenth Avenue North and "It's Not Over Yet" by the Australian brothers of For King & Country. While scanning a list of my favorites, these titles humbly called out and drew me in.

Worn

The song "Worn" captures the emotions of lead singer and guitarist Mike Donehey. He and his wife were exhausted from sleepless nights with a second newborn baby, all the while going through a huge misunderstanding with a friend. During an interview, the band members explain the song's message. They assert that people appreciate when you speak freely about your true feelings because they can relate with what's going on in their own lives. Most of us "live in the tension of begging for redemption to win, and believing that it will, but not necessarily seeing that."

Another great point the band makes is that when others have moments of suffering, we shouldn't always feel the need to immediately provide answers. As they testify, "before Jesus fixed us, He felt us." Yes, Jesus saved the world, but first he experienced life as a human to better understand what we endure. Romans 12:15 says, "Be happy with those who are happy, and weep with those who weep." We are called to simply be present—as an ear to listen or a shoulder to cry on. God will spiritually heal at the appropriate time, but we are meant to be His hands of physical comfort.

Mike shares a more universal meaning from a sermon he heard. He symbolizes earth as a garment all laid out, and in some places, a bit worn through. Christ's redemptive work reweaves that fabric, which we should help with. He says our job is to "bring the kingdom of God social justice, forgiveness, love, peace, shalom"; we *get* to do it.

It's Not Over Yet

According to Luke and Joel Smallbone of For King & Country, "It's Not Over Yet" was written for those who believe something they've experienced rules their lives, leaving them with a sort of "doomsday" attitude. The two were inspired to write this when their younger sister was diagnosed with Lyme disease. This song is meant to be "a spurring on, an edification, and encouragement" for their sister, as well as us, to resist the feeling of wanting to give it all up. This dynamic duo urges us to remain positive in dark times and believe we will get through our struggles, coming out stronger as a result. "Keep on fighting out of the dark into the light. Never give up, never give in: It's not over."

You Are Not Alone

Let's dig into the powerfully moving lyrics in these two songs. Am I'm talking to someone today who is bruised and beaten? Do you hear a voice that says you won't get past this one? Are you tired and worn? Do you feel defeated? Is your heart heavy from the work it takes to keep on breathing? Does your soul feel crushed by the weight of this world? Are your prayers wearing thin? Are you crying out with all that you have left? Are you worn even before the day begins? Have you hit your limit? Have you lost your will to fight?"

Even these Christian men who spend their lives singing for Jesus have moments of weakness. Allow their vulnerability and honesty to resonate and meet you in your suffering. Acknowledge and express your raw emotions. These lyrics confirm that it is okay, and even normal, to have these feelings. You are not alone.

My Cloud and Its Silver Lining

I can readily transport myself into the heart of these verses when I recall my past. The ugly, unrelenting monster of depression plagued me during bouts of relationship heartache and a career crisis. Darkness surrounded me and strangled my sense of reasoning; I was full of doom and gloom, rejection, and hopelessness. When life demanded my appearance, I mustered just enough energy to get out of bed and put one foot in front of the other. Simply getting through each of those days was my only focus. I kept praying and fighting to believe my struggles wouldn't last forever. It was during those bleak moments I began to fully grasp God's goodness in the presence and support of my circle of family and friends. Prayers, phone calls, emails, text messages, and surprise visits were all monumental in my recovery. I clung to every positive and encouraging word deposited in my account. In my state of mind, I may not have completely agreed with the optimistic comments that seemed out of reach, but I tried to convince myself they were right. They were; I just couldn't see it yet.

As added assurance, God used Josh Wilson's "Before the Morning" to speak to me. "'Cause the pain that you've been feeling—it can't compare to the joy that's coming" was the inspirational mantra my soul needed to hear. Seriously, I just kept repeating those words to myself. The notion of a future joy that could trump my current feelings allowed me to visualize a way out of my misery. I discovered what "chaos" really means: **C**hrist **H**as **A**n **O**utcome **S**oon.

According to Matthew 17:20, all you need is faith the size of a mustard seed. K-LOVE was my musical morsel of hope. The radio station's claim to fame is playing the right song, at the right moment, for the right person. I publicly add my testimonial. As equally impactful as the melodious messages on the air are the uplifting stories, contagious energy, and overall ministry the whole God-fearing team contributes. Thirty days of nothing but K-LOVE radio *will* change your life.

Gaining Strength from Others

From day one of tuning in to this radio station, you will quickly realize that not one of us is free from trouble; that's the reality of the world we live in. Just as sure as we rise to our feet each morning, we will fall to our knees in mourning every so often. We all face our own battles; Christians cry, too—deeply and often. And I won't lie to you: Your worries won't magically vanish the instant you call on Christ. There will still be storms in your life. Tenth Avenue North, For King & Country, and I can attest to that statement. God doesn't promise us incessant health and happiness here; our reward is reserved for heaven. While tears will continue to fall, rest assured in God's message from John 16:33: "I have told you all this so that you may have peace in me. Here on earth you will have many trials and sorrows. But take heart, because I have overcome the world."

Many people you come across each day are going through similar, and perhaps even deeper, levels of adversity. I plead with you to swallow your pride, tear down your walls, and open your heart. Invest your time and effort in personally getting to know others; everyone has a story. Don't forget to share yours. You may be surprised by the rough terrain many have traveled to arrive where they are. Truly listen to fully appreciate their resolve in overcoming past hardships and offer support for the burdens they carry. Gain strength through their testament of perseverance. Day after day, I strive to deepen my relationships and make a point to spiritually grow through each conversation. Correspondingly, I become more and more astonished how past heartbreak is melted away by a Christ-filled glow. I love seeing the radiant smile that proudly proclaims one's identity as a redeemed child of the Most High.

Perhaps you consider yourself lacking in, uncertain of, or lost in your faith—yet neither of the perspectives I've presented speak to you. Import your ambiguity, curiosity, doubt, mistrust, anxiety, or resentment, and deliberate your reasoning for giving up on God. Maybe you've been tackling each day on your own for so long, you can't even remember when life started spiraling out of control. You might be embarrassed of who you've become. It's likely been years since you've spoken to God. If God has felt far away for a long time, just know that He's not the one who moved. The great thing about a relationship is that it takes two to tango; furthermore, both parties have a say. You may have given up on God, but He's still the president of your fan club and continues to pursue you with reckless abandon.

It's Redemption Season

If I have permission to be frank ("No, you're Matt") for a minute, you've given up too early. It doesn't matter how far you have fallen; Jesus still says, "Come." You don't have to fix yourself before He will accept you. As Crowder sings, "Come as you are," and allow God to take care of the rest. Be encouraged by the heartfelt advice of For King & Country. They are right; "it's not over yet," and "it's redemption season." In fact, if you are ready to receive Christ for the first time, your life is only beginning. None of that heartache, misfortune, or failure matters anymore. You may wonder how God will ever forgive you, but He will; in fact, He already has. It's about time you start forgiving yourself. Leave behind whatever enchains you, let go, and free yourself. When you let Jesus conquer your demons, you will see the fruition of your dreams.

Come with the rest of us to the foot of the cross for His unlimited mercy. Just like Hillsong United's "Touch the Sky" proclaims, you will find your life when you lay it down. Give it to God. As Tenth Avenue North offers: He can give you rest. He wants to wash away all your sins and bestow on you a new life full of countless blessings.

My calling is to encourage you to re-establish your relationship with Him. I firmly believe I hold a piece of your future in my heart; I'm desperately working to help you become aware of your potential. Remember that your unique mission is between you and your Creator. Nurture your prayer life to discover His specific desires for you. Include an adequate amount of time for listening, rather than just submitting a laundry list of requests to Him. Here's the thing: *He* knows what *you* want; *you* don't know what *He* wants.

Once you receive His counsel, follow through with the next critical step: Act on it. Follow the advice in Matthew West's song "Do Something" and realize that "we're never gonna change the world by standing still." Yes, God will do His part, but don't forget to do yours.

By the same token, don't forget Who you are doing your part for. It's not for you anymore; it's all for the greater glory of God. As I've learned from the Bible, God quickly humbles the proud. Philippians 4:13 states, "For I can do everything through Christ, who gives me strength." I've been educated on the true meaning of these words and how they are often misinterpreted. This declaration shouldn't give you false confidence of having the ability to fly in the sky or the strength to hurl a train, nor does it bestow magic on you to complete your midterm paper while fast asleep or reclaim a lost TV remote without getting off the couch (unless it's hidden in the cushions, like ours usually is.) Here's a more practical explanation for this verse: When you insist on fighting against your heavenly Father's will, you limit yourself from ever reaching the pinnacle of Maslow's pyramid (as you recall from chapter 1). However, when you dial in to what God has in store, you can do everything with Him by your side. Matthew 10:39 further supports this stance: "If you cling to your life, you will lose it; but if you give up your life for me, you will find it." Your future lies in that difference. Let Him work in your life. Better yet, get lost in Him. You will start to find meaning, purpose, and an understanding of what it means to be a child of God. In your ongoing journey of faith, thirst for knowledge, yearn for understanding, and seek the truth.

Start today. Devote your whole heart to this new life. You will be utterly amazed by the resulting outpouring of grace. As the Good Book calls for in Luke 6:38, "Give, and you will receive. Your gift will return to you in full—pressed down, shaken together to make room for more, running over, and poured into your lap. The amount you give will determine the amount you get back." I used to associate this doctrine only with monetary transactions. As my spiritual awareness heightens, I am beginning to fully appreciate Luke's intent to include all aspects of our giving. Sure, tithing is an important discipline to practice, but this verse encompasses all your time, talents, and treasures.

Chapter 15

THROUGH MY HAZEL EYES

Perspective Three: Why We All Need God

I'd like to invite you to watch the world through my hazel eyes. As for me and my perspective, I will be the first to admit that I haven't earned a pedestal to stand on, by any means. I'm not a church leader who regularly occupies a pulpit with the eager ears of a congregation. I'm certainly not, and will never claim to be, the Billy Graham of this generation. I'm more of a Moses in my own right, as I frequently stumble in speech. I haven't lived a near-death experience like one of my best friends, nor can I share in my dad's agony of actually conversing with the devil (which still makes the hair stand up on his skin every time he tells that story).

So who am I? I'm a thirty-two-year-old who already notices a receding hairline and reluctantly reveals lasting scars from the not-so-kind teenage acne years. I'm a guy who always seems to be in constant thought, a simple man who loves to write and bring out emotions in others. I guess what I am trying to say is, I'm average. I haven't been granted any superpowers, although I did once have myself convinced I was in the first stages of transforming into Spiderman. One morning after putting on my glasses, my vision was blurry. Upon removing the glasses, my world turned clear. I went back and forth for a while—blurry, clear, blurry, clear, blurry ... you get the gist. I wasn't shooting webs out of my wrists yet, so I tried to rein in my excitement. Moments later, I realized I had merely slept in my contacts the night before. So you see, average, and a little dimwitted at that.

I put my pants on one leg at a time, like everyone else. However, I dress with the intentions addressed in Ephesians 6:13–18:

> Therefore, put on every piece of God's armor so you will be able to resist the enemy in the time of evil. Then after the battle you will still be standing firm. Stand your ground, putting on the belt of truth and the body armor of God's righteousness. For shoes, put on the peace that comes from the Good News so that you will be fully prepared. In addition to all of these, hold up the shield of faith to stop the fiery arrows of the devil. Put on salvation as your helmet, and take the sword of the Spirit, which is the word of God. Pray in the Spirit at all times and on every occasion. Stay alert and be persistent in your prayers for all believers everywhere.

While this attire may not be considered cool or win me any popularity contests, it's my predawn activity that might cause many nonbelievers' eyebrows to raise. Learning from my spiritual mentors, I now make it a daily goal—still falling short—to visit our family prayer room (or *War Room*, depending on if you have seen this life-changing movie yet). Striving to deepen my relationship in solitude with my heavenly Father, I also use this time to mentally prepare myself for the day ahead of me. I can never predict the challenges I will encounter once I walk out that front door; I simply trust and rely on being properly suited in my faith. Having endured days of immense tragedies and triumphant victories, my valleys are never too low nor my peaks too high that I lose a sense of God's presence beside me.

One of my strongest convictions for writing this book is to reach nonbelievers who may not otherwise accept Jesus. Am I talking to someone today who needs encouragement? Do you feel like you continually fall short? Put it right there, pal; I can't get through one day without sinning. Have you been called unworthy and told you can't live up to certain religious expectations? Guess what: You don't have to. Were you led to believe that because of your past, you are ruined, too far gone, or lost forever? Boy, do I have some mighty good news for you: God says you are special, valuable, and always worth saving.

The Truth Is in His Word

Although learning how to become a follower of Christ can be complicated and overwhelming at times, thankfully, we are furnished with the necessary guidebook. Here are a few handpicked, clear-cut gems from God's word:

- "Jesus replied, 'I tell you the truth, unless you are born again, you cannot see the Kingdom of God'" (John 3:3).
- "For this is how God loved the world: He gave his one and only Son, so that everyone who believes in him will not perish but have eternal life" (John 3:16).
- "Jesus told him, 'I am the way, the truth, and the life. No one can come to the Father except through me'" (John 14:6).
- "God saved you by his grace when you believed. And you can't take credit for this; it is a gift from God. Salvation is not a reward for the good things we have done, so none of us can boast about it" (Ephesians 2:8–9).

Connecting the dots, we can use these verses collectively as a roadmap to understanding salvation. To truly believe involves a spiritual dying of one's self, followed by a new spring of life in Christ, knowing that it's not earned through your own works, but rather by accepting His gift of an eternity in heaven. Despite the literary explanation, what proves challenging is the day-to-day habits of actually living out His instructions. For those with a short attention span, I will save you the confusion of reading the hundreds of laws in the Old Testament, or Torah, if you can remember Jesus' two most important commandments (Mt. 22:37, 39).

- "You must love the Lord your God with all your heart, all your soul, and all your mind."
- "Love your neighbor as yourself."

Jesus simplifies the complex set of rules of His day in Matthew 22:40: "The entire law and all the demands of the prophets are based on these two commandments." The same two principles can easily be used to filter conflicting information and realign our mindset with God's in today's world.

My Solemn Oath

What do I consider my personal *musts* as one of Jesus' disciples? First and foremost, I *must* believe He is Who He says He is: the one true God. I *must* not worship or serve any other gods. I *must* give Him sole credit for creation of the universe. I *must* have confidence that God came to earth in human flesh as His son, Jesus Christ. I *must* acknowledge Jesus' sacrifice on the cross. I *must* appreciate the love in His sacrifice and realize He redeemed all my sins. I *must* accept God's personal invitation to me and establish a relationship with Him. I *must* trust that Jesus is my Savior and has a place waiting for me in heaven.

The second commandment insists I love my neighbor as myself. An easy way for me to accomplish this is to simply live by the Golden Rule. If you recall from chapter 1, I was born an innately self-centered creature. I must voluntarily undergo a transformation in order to adopt an altruistic lifestyle. My calling as a Christian compels me to revolt against that covetous instinct. Life is not about me anymore; it is about Him. As Matthew 16:24 states, "Then Jesus said to his disciples, 'If any of you wants to be my follower, you must give up your own way, take up your cross, and follow me.'" God desires me to lift the focus off myself, utilize my strengths, and direct them into a purpose of improving the lives of His children. I continually fight a battle of opposing forces: The world and my head constantly tempt me to blurt out, "Give me," while Jesus and my heart patiently and calmly offer, "Give thee."

Chapter 16

CAN YOU EVEN IMAGINE?

Perspective Four: From God's Throne

*O*kay, I'm obviously not going to do this perspective justice, but God knows full well my intentions, so I will continue. For just a brief moment, let's all hypothetically strap on the heavenly sandals (although who knows; maybe He is rocking some sweet Nikes). You are God, the Creator. You possess all the keys. You control the master circuit board; better yet, you *are* the master circuit board. Let those earth-shattering thoughts sink in for a minute.

How would you make things different? What would be your first order of business? Would you allow free will or force the best decisions (in your opinion) on your people? Where, when, and how often would you perform miracles? Would you practice favoritism or grant every prayer request?

The movie *Bruce Almighty* was produced around this very concept of adamantly believing we can step in and improve overall order. Actor Jim Carrey's character's wish came true after much complaining about the way God was running the show. Suffice to say that Bruce wasn't prepared for the chaos that ensued. He was quickly hit with a reality check that the grass is not always greener on the other side, as we so often presume—especially in this case, when the other side is responsible for the entire human race.

Let's turn back the clock and revisit the blueprint days, with you above the heavens with the powerful rod and staff in hand. In the beginning, you created man and woman, with the ultimate intention of living with them in perfect unity and harmony. Because of the devil's enticement, along with Adam and Eve's original sin, your plan drastically changed. Evil entered this world and continued to cause corruption and wreak havoc from that point forward.

Meanwhile, you vacated a perfect kingdom. You could have merely observed from above without any intervention. You did not; that's not the type of leader you wanted your people to serve. Instead, you took off your glistening white robe and boldly came down to earth in our human image as Jesus Christ to show us how to live. You were present in flesh, not only as an example, but as *the* example of agape love, for thirty-three years. True to your mysterious nature, you envisioned that the only way to save the world and accomplish universal salvation—should we chose to accept—was through your incomparable mercy and grace. You carried the weight of theft, adultery, abuse, murder, and all other injustices on your shoulders, in the form of a Roman cross on your way to Calvary. With the power to escape the agony and torture at any moment, you bravely and consciously continued to endure the crucifixion. All you ask in return from your followers is acknowledgment of your existence, thankfulness for your sacrifice, and acceptance of a relationship. They can punch their ticket to heaven by simply believing in your extraordinary measures. What an amazing bargain you offer to mankind, huh?

Now that you have theoretically sat on the royal throne, delivered commands in a deep, booming voice, and temporarily possessed the world in the palm of your hand, aren't you thankful you don't actually have to make all those impossibly hard decisions? Out of deep respect and reverence for the true God, I'm revoking your rod and staff privileges, thereby quickly truncating this section. A positional power of that magnitude bears an overwhelming amount of responsibility that we can't even pretend to fully assume.

Chapter 17

DIVIDING THE ROOM: NONBELIEVERS

$\mathcal{M}$y friends in the first two perspectives both grew up knowing God. They attended regular worship throughout childhood but then proceeded to fall out of favor, for different reasons. As these are just a couple of the many angles on faith, I realize we have all come to this point with different upbringings and personal convictions. Maybe you are reading this, having neither stepped foot inside a sanctuary nor been introduced to God. Perhaps life's travels have left you with a crushed soul in search of guidance. Regardless of your background, I think we all need to gain a better understanding of who God really is.

God Is Love

I want to unravel another layer within those two commandments Jesus gave in the book of Matthew. We are instructed to love God, our neighbor, and ourselves. What does it mean to love God? You might have heard the saying, "God is love." What is love? In our Western culture, we *love* many pleasures: shopping sprees, decadent desserts, and cable television. We also love luxuries like remote-start and heated leather seats, while sipping on a venti-double-espresso-skinny-extra whip-half-sweet-mocha-frappusomething on a cold winter's day. Our society may appreciate and enjoy these wants (not needs) and comforts, but we are losing sight of the type of love in reference here.

According to the ancient Greek, there are four different types of love, none of which refer to a fondness for shopping, food, entertainment, or luxury:

- *Eros*: romantic or passionate love; a primal instinct
- *Phileo*: brotherly or sisterly love for a close friend or confidant
- *Storge*: familial love for spouse, child, parent, or close sibling
- *Agape*: God's incomparable love for us

We can each likely find someone in our lives as an example of eros, phileo, and storge love. However, no matter how strong our storge love may be for another, there is no parallel to God's love for us. Agape love is explained in 1 Corinthians 13:4–8 (adapted a bit):

> God's love is patient and kind. *We grow impatient and cruel.* God's love is not jealous or boastful or proud or rude. *We are envious, arrogant, and inconsiderate.* God's love does not demand its own way. *We are narrow-minded and self-seeking.* God's love is not irritable, and it keeps no record of being wronged. *We are moody and hold grudges.* God's love does not rejoice about injustice but rejoices whenever the truth wins out. *We consistently smudge the line of right and wrong.* God's love never gives up, never loses faith, is always hopeful, and endures through every circumstance. *We often give up, lack faith, lose hope, and bow out early.* God's love lasts forever. *We fall out of love.*

Are you starting to get the idea? God's love for us is unlike anything we can imagine. Paul pleads to us in Ephesians 3:18, "And may you have the power to understand, as all God's people should, how wide, how long, how high, and how deep his love is." His love is sacrificial, unconditional, infinite, unwavering, perfect, and pure.

We did nothing for Him, yet He gave everything for us. God's heart is wonderfully captured in a Matthew Kelly video entitled "What If It Were Your Only Son?" This emotionally stirring piece is most definitely worth the six minutes and eight seconds of your life, as it paints a picture of what God's selfless love would look like in today's world. Kelly's Australian accent alone will captivate you. *(Please stop and watch this video; have tissues handy.)*

If that scenario became a reality today, what would you do as the parent of that little boy? How would you respond to a doctor begging for all of your son's blood? If your answer is no, we would continue to drop like flies. If your answer is yes, you would make it possible for the rest of mankind to live, but you would have to watch your son die. The good news is that you don't have to make that gut-wrenching decision; He already did. Every time I listen to that unmistakable reminder of God's love, bittersweet tears of mourning and thankfulness flood my eyes. How can we hate, ignore, or undermine that kind of love?

Interviewing God

Please keep in mind that there is only enough room for one ruler in your heart. It's up to you to decide who or what that will be: God, pride, money, possessions, lust, and so on. Perhaps you have previously hired other candidates, but no one seems to be getting the job done; there is still an aching, undeniable void. As we continue through this chapter, ask yourself if any other options measure up to what God brings to the table. Hold all your calls, cancel your afternoon plans, and prepare yourself for the last interview you will likely ever hold.

Let's examine God's bio. Our Father established selflessness, patented sacrifice, and initiated humility. He responds to many different titles that express His power: the Alpha and the Omega, King of kings, Lord of lords, El Shaddai, and the Great I Am. In the same breath, He also answers to Abba, indicative of the intimate relationship He desires to share with each of us.

Moving along, we see God has quite the work experience. His initiative was put on display in Genesis 1 during those six particular days He created the heavens and the earth: day and night; sky and sea; land and vegetation; sun, moon, and stars; animals; and mankind. Let's appreciate this miraculous feat for a minute. Next time you are in a rush out the door and already focused on your upcoming endeavor, stop and smell the roses. Mindfully step outside and thank Him for as far as your eyes can see—and beyond. Get lost and be still amongst the scenery around you. Beautiful, isn't it? A wise friend once suggested to me, "If you ultimately desire to have a greater appreciation for God, cherish nature and experience His creation firsthand." Yet of all the accomplishments on God's resume, He would surely whisper, "*You* are the one of which I am most proud."

Making Sense of It All

I apologize if your brain is on overload. Let's rein in this theoretical talk and incorporate some of these new concepts into your everyday life. Allow me to politely, yet intently, tug at your heartstrings. Close your eyes and briefly call to mind your most dreadful moments. Do you remember your emotions the night you caught your husband of twenty years under the sheets with another woman? How did you feel the morning you were falsely accused of murder and escorted to incarceration? How did you react when you received the call of your teenage daughter's attempted suicide? What were your thoughts as you held your lifeless baby boy in your arms? I realize these scenarios may seem far-fetched and extreme to many, but they are no doubt still fresh in the minds of those who have actually lived these agonizing realities. Regardless of the level of intensity, we can all agree our worst days have the ability to lock us in a corrosive state of mind.

When you experience uncertainty, disappointment, anxiety, anger, heartbreak, betrayal, or hopelessness, how do you maintain control of your emotions, push through, and keep propelling forward? In whom or what do you take comfort? Where do you place your trust? How do you find hope?

I believe the most adept person to cool your jets or warm your heart is someone who has faced the same afflictions. Many may offer their condolences and support, but the real assurance of knowing you can move on and one day smile again is found in the eyes of someone who has overcome your situation. I can think of no one more qualified than the thirty-three-year-old Man Who accepted, withstood, and eventually conquered all the suffering of the world. There is nothing you will ever encounter that He hasn't already claimed victory over.

Doubting Thomases

I'm sure there are many of you who remain skeptical of a higher power. Have you ever had situations in your life that couldn't be reasonably explained? A fitting example, which hits very close to home, was when one of my best friends (Remember Nick?) collapsed during a 5K run in our hometown. In fact, his heart actually stopped beating for nearly ten minutes. After failed attempts of resuscitation, he spontaneously and miraculously recovered without any brain damage or lasting effects, which still stumps the medical world to this day. By the grace of God and Fr. Kapaun's intercession, he was able to stand by my side as a groomsman in our wedding. I send him a kid's birthday card every year to celebrate his new life; this year, he turned six.

You may very well have your own life-changing event one day, which may lead to an initiation or deepening of your faith. The rest of you might not be recipients of that same fortune. We all lead different lives, but one thing is sure: God works in mysterious ways. That's why I believe it's so important to make faith special and personal to you, not necessarily falling in line with others' expectations. Don't get me wrong, a church family is a wonderful asset I strongly recommend, but don't place all your focus on the rituals of religion; invest in a relationship with your heavenly Father. Expend effort studying the scriptures, as well as learning from mentors similar to the ones encouraged earlier. Expand your horizons and unearth various resources on Christianity. I recommend the Bible study guide

Making Sense of the Bible by Adam Hamilton and the novel *The Shack* by Wm. Paul Young, which will independently meet you outside the box and help you explore beyond the norm. The movie *God's Not Dead 2* highlights three books that focus on the inarguable facts of Christianity: *Man, Myth, Messiah* by Rice Broocks, *The Case for Christ* by Lee Strobel, and *Cold Case Christianity* by J. Warner Wallace. They have certainly piqued my interest; I hope curiosity will also put them in your lap.

Maybe literary works aren't chicken soup for your soul. If you happen to be more of a movie aficionado, two incredible reminders of God's greatness, along with the aforementioned *God's Not Dead,* are the films *Courageous* and *War Room.* Cinematic production is meant to draw emotion, and these two inspirational pieces don't disappoint. Let them ignite your flame for the King of kings.

Hopefully throughout your exploration of faith, you will realize that God won't ever compare your credentials to those of your boss, pastor, friend, rival, prisoner on death row, or even to incredibly selfless figures like Saint Mother Teresa or Chaplain Emil Kapaun. Neither volunteer work and prayer time, nor a lack of cursing and stealing, can earn us real estate in paradise. While we are made in the image and likeness of God, we are all a far cry from perfection. Actually, we as believers and nonbelievers are more alike in our weaknesses than our strengths. We share the same burdens, sufferings, tragedies, and failures. The difference between God-followers and skeptics is that no matter how often our sinful natures manifest, believers embody a deep and abiding peace. We know there is a Father Who readily accepts us as we are and comforts us with His unconditional love.

Others have their testimonials, and I have mine. Now let's create yours. If you already feel God moving inside you, put down this book and don't let me stop you. If you need a little more direction, these suggestions may provide fertile ground to help your faith-filled roots grow:

- Volunteer regularly.
- Get involved in a local church.

- Open the Bible and become familiar with it.
- Seek out a spiritual mentor you respect and admire.
- Open your eyes, ears, and heart for God's guidance.
- Initiate an accountability group with close friends you trust.
- Visit newspring.org and watch Pastor Mark Hoover or Associate Pastor Jonathan Hoover deliver God's word.
- Tune in to the nearest K-LOVE radio station and take the Thirty-Day Challenge of listening only to Christian radio for a month.

Chapter 18

DIVIDING THE ROOM: BELIEVERS

_I_s God alive within your heart? Do you know what His mission is for you? I honestly believe God handed me my mission over four years ago. Slow at times, but sure to the end, I've been working tirelessly to formulate and organize the right words to spread His message and enlist more soldiers for God's army. Please join me; let's rally the troops and set this world on fire. Here's our battle plan:

Objective 1: Be more inviting and compassionate toward nonbelievers.
Objective 2: Weave the thread of God into our daily lives.
Objective 3: Fight together, not against one another.
Objective 4: Bring everyone Home with us.

Be More Inviting and Compassionate toward Nonbelievers

One of the more popular reasons for skepticism or even resentment toward Christ is the inferiority outsiders feel from regular churchgoers. But have we ever really taken the time to question why they don't join in? Let's ask, openly listen, and use their responses to better understand their view of the stained-glass windows. We, as God's universal congregation, must set a resolution to make guests feel more welcome. Be careful not to suffocate or attack them like fresh meat, but certainly don't ignore or alienate them. Otherwise, why would they want to return—besides the free coffee and doughnuts? Getting others in the door to hear a message from God's word is our first advancement. In order to grow our Christian family, we should be projecting our focus on those *outside* the church. On a weekly basis, I eagerly receive orders from Pastors Mark and Jonathan (serving as lieutenant general and colonel, respectively, who answer to our sovereign five-star General) to spread God's love and be His liaison for the lost and lonely.

Weave the Thread of God into Our Daily Lives

Onward we march. Allow your faith to shine in the modern world. Don't be a convenient Christian; bring church with you—wherever you go. Let the you who is present throughout the workweek be recognizable to the you who attends weekend worship. Many perceive the spiritual and secular world to be of different animals, but that's where we go wrong. Why can't they be interwoven as threads of our daily lives? Mike Donehey from Tenth Avenue North explains it best in the universal message behind his song "Worn": Christ is the fabric, and we are His able and willing hands that are to reweave Him back into our tapestry of society. We live in a broken world that needs major repairing. It's time we—as Christ's weavers—start mending the frays, tears, stains, and holes of mankind.

As we learned in chapter 3, pastors are not the only holy beacons meant to set an example and spread the Good News. We don't all stand behind pulpits, but that shouldn't limit our impact. (This was a life-changing revelation for me.) Offering a different form of preaching to your audience may produce surprisingly successful results. In fact, your efforts may be better received in lieu of a religious figure, because of your stronger existing relationship and everyday presence. You see, you can make a dramatic difference. The magnificent Helen Keller showed awareness of her potential with these infamous words: "I am only one, but still I am one. I cannot do everything, but still I can do something; and because I cannot do everything, I will not refuse to do something that I can do." Each one of us is called in an individual way to be His messenger. No matter your life situation, opportunity lies before you. Utilize your position as the pedestal it is to affirm the greatness of God.

Fight Together, Not against One Another

Learning from Helen Keller, we must realize our full potential, band together, and invest in the same cause. With God leading the charge, we will be a dominant and dynamic force. Currently, we are a liability against our own efforts. We are too busy trying to outdo or one-up our siblings (we are all God's children—are we not?) to appreciate the fact that we all have our eyes on the same prize. We need to start fighting for and with our brothers and sisters, not against them. From what I've learned in scripture, Christ doesn't play favorites. If you research the life of Jesus in the Gospels, notice where He spent the majority of His days. He wasn't found celebrating or parading around with the cream of the crop; He was serving, healing, and ministering to the sick, poor, and lame. We place too much emphasis on the trivial factors that alienate us and not enough on the One Who unites us.

Let's ask ourselves these questions: Does our indefinite home depend on a rightly chosen religion or denomination? Do we have to attend the church adorned by a certain steeple to earn entrance past Saint Peter? Must our services flow a certain way or our religious leaders don a specific garment? Is it essential we always dress in our Sunday best?

No, not likely, nope, nah. Honestly, I am ecstatic when I see overflowing parking lots at all the churches throughout town. The enlightening truth is that the word "church" actually defines a group of people, not a particular building. As Matthew 18:20 declares, "For where two or three gather together as my followers, I am there among them." While a sanctuary or chapel is a wonderful location for worship, God's presence transcends man-made structures. The Holy Spirit possesses the unique ability to fill any and all venues simultaneously—often making house calls, copiloting road trips, and attending concerts. My wife and I once attended a nontraditional Friday evening praise and worship session in an industrial basement. Was Christ any less present in that moment than at a traditional Sunday gathering? Witnessing the deep desire and yearning in the worshipers' hearts for God's love to permeate the room that night helps me confidently shake my head to the contrary. *Where* we worship isn't nearly as important as *Who* we worship.

Now, while I am by no means urging you to leave your congregation, I do want you to know that frequenting a pew once a week doesn't automatically qualify you for heaven. I fall in line with Christian singer Matthew West, who is living and breathing the word. He acknowledges this truth: "The thing is, dressing up, going to church, dropping a twenty in the offering plate; those things are all well and good, but that doesn't make you a Christian." Going through the motions might fool the common man, but God sees beyond the curtain of your heart. After all, the Pharisees appeared as the quintessential symbol of divinity on the outside— animal sacrifices, fasting, offerings, tithes, priestly garments, and so on. Yet beyond their well-concealed disguise, they lacked the key ingredients of righteousness and love. The Pharisees weren't all wrong; the surrendering nature of certain disciplines (fasting, tithing, offerings, etc.) certainly carry weight in our spiritual maturation. But above all, we must never forget the verb within the greatest two commandments—love. According to The Beatles and 1 Corinthians, all you need is love, and everything else is useless or meaningless without its presence.

Bring Everyone Home with Us

"By your Spirit make us one with Christ, one with each other, and one in ministry to all the world, until Christ comes in final victory and we feast at His Heavenly banquet." Hearing that last line during communion preparation at my hometown Methodist church always gave me goosebumps. We know our Father is patiently saving a place for all of us. The telling question is, how many is *us* going to be? God is the Host of all hosts, so the more, the merrier, in His eyes. His table has been prepared with more than enough chairs for all His children, should each one accept His dinner invitation.

That's where we come into play. Matthew 5:14 calls us to do more in our discipleship: "You are the light of the world—like a city on a hilltop that cannot be hidden." Christians, assemble. Our assignment is to hand out RSVPs and fill His seats. We must sign, seal, and deliver them as soon as possible. No one knows if it will be today, tomorrow, or two thousand years from now, but one day, the rapture will become a reality. Pay heed to the announcement from Matthew 24:44: "You also must be ready all the time, for the Son of Man will come when least expected." Don't let family, friends, or anyone around you miss their opportunity. We are encouraged, nay, called to follow Jesus' lead by preaching to any and all, wherever we go. Let's make it our unified mission to leave no man, woman, or child behind. Who's with me?

Chapter 19

STRIVING FOR JESUS

My Incessant Search for Betterment

$\mathscr{I}$ sincerely hope I haven't portrayed myself as one who has life all figured out. Then again, who does? (If you are the one who's successfully managed to find all the right pieces to your puzzle, I'm on the first plane out.) Until I find you, I will just keep putting one Christ-led foot in front of the other, asking God to show me the light to see the next step and instill in me the courage to take it. I wouldn't mind a little wisdom, to boot. There's a "metamotivation" component deep within that keeps me striving for constant betterment; I desperately want to reach the summit of Maslow's hierarchy of needs: self-actualization. More importantly, I live to hear God one day say, "Well done, my good and faithful servant."

I have the following memory in my mind on repeat: Pastor Mark once spoke of a conversation at his grandfather's deathbed. His grandfather, while looking intently at loved ones he was moments from leaving, passed on this bit of advice that still haunts Mark—and now me—to this day: "I have finally figured out the right way to live, and now it's time to die." I'm still anxiously anticipating those initial words to come across my lips and praying the epiphany occurs in my thirties, instead of on my way out. I earnestly feel I am getting closer each day, with inevitable setbacks on occasion. However, there is still so much that I must learn.

There are a vast number of avenues to knowing God more intimately. The ideas I am about to share with you are not magical steps that guarantee an immediate extinguishing of all your problems. All the same, I will offer a concise glimpse of what I consider to be integral factors that have aided me in maturing as a Christian and sharpening my focus on Jesus. I pray this insight will invigorate your soul and encourage you to take advantage of similar resources. I hope you feel empowered and poised to start sprinting up your staircase of spiritual growth.

Building a Band of Brothers

After poring over *The Resolution for Men*, I gathered some of the best Christian men I know to start a weekly Bible study and accountability group; we called ourselves Men under Construction. This band of brothers has since joined forces to become members of the holy wildfire that is Kapaun's Men (fatherkapaun.org). Like Proverbs 27:17 encourages, "As iron sharpens iron, so a friend sharpens a friend." I would happily go to battle with and for these men.

Exploring His Word

Thanks to the convenience of the Holy Bible application and its one-year reading plan, I accomplished a lifelong goal of reading God's word in its entirety. Spending fifteen to twenty minutes daily in scripture was instrumental to my spiritual health. While I still can't readily quote the Bible word for word, I have the foundation I have always wanted. After reading His story, I know He loves us, and I know it's my job, and furthermore, my privilege to spread that message.

Giving Back

Holly and I have enjoyed the privilege of spiritually and financially providing for a child from Sierra Leone through the great organization of World Vision. Being a small part of something bigger allows you to look outside your own four walls. We also felt extremely fortunate when our good friend asked us to assist with a high school confirmation class. Helping influence and mold young minds was a powerful reminder of the opportunities we have before us. We gave our time, but we received so much more in return. God has a funny way of making that happen. (Remember Lk. 6:38?)

Devoting Time to Daily Prayer

As part of an intercessory group at our church, I have been a prayer warrior for those in need. These requests quickly put things in perspective and allow me to shrug off the minor irritations of life that are really only first-world problems. Being late to work, having a flat tire, or getting berated by a customer doesn't carry enough weight to constitute a bad day in my eyes. When I pray over the concerning matters of eviction, cancer, abuse, divorce, suicide, or a lost soul, the heartbreak I feel overshadows any thoughts of my own suffering. I have learned that when my eyes are fixed outside myself, Jesus smiles.

Growing a Family of Faith

In becoming more involved and joining a small group at church, my family and I have surrounded ourselves with some extraordinary disciples of Christ. I greatly anticipate Sunday evenings where we gather to strengthen our faith and friendship. Immersing myself in the weekly company of these men and women, who infuse wisdom and instill courage, has been an absolute game changer in my spiritual journey. To grow in my faith with like minds, and to know my kids are being influenced in the same manner, leaves me with a peace that is beyond words.

Investing in People, Not Stuff

I continually try to avert my gaze from the pleasures of this world and rid my mind-set of wanting the next big thing. After all, it's just stuff that will be left behind someday. Singer-songwriter Kristian Bush is right on the money: You never see a hearse with a trailer hitch. As a result, I push myself to place more emphasis on people, rather than stuff, by initiating and building lasting relationships.

Feasting on Soul Sugar

I fiercely feed off quotes—as you can see throughout this book—to bolster my inspiration for God. I pass by a Baptist church on my daily commute and reap the benefits of their marquee reader board. (I actually tracked down the responsible party and sung my praises for the positive and meaningful impact he has made in my life.) I have been using these messages as my weekly ammunition to make a difference in the community. Here are some of my favorites:

- Be a witness.
- The Bible is best used open.
- Worrying is praying to the wrong god.
- It's far better to have God approve than people applaud.
- God takes you as you are, but never leaves you that way.
- Every temptation is just another opportunity to trust God.
- Peace is not the absence of trouble, but the presence of God.
- You don't have to know the way when you stay close to the One Who does.

Chapter 20

FAITH AT ITS FINEST

I thrive when witnessing the passion and strength my fellow brothers and sisters exude for Christ, especially when they are faced with devastating hardships under which others would crumble. I have collected an overwhelming number of examples over the years, but here are the memories of three powerful testimonies I deeply cherish:

Forgiveness for All to See

The first example was televised nationwide, when Oklahoma City Thunder's former Assistant Coach Monty Williams delivered the eulogy at his wife's funeral with incomprehensible strength. In listening to him preach (that's what he was doing), I heard a line I will never forget. Many had been reaching out to offer condolences and give sympathy for his loss. Monty's response was perfect: "We didn't lose her. When you lose something, you can't find it. I know exactly where my wife is." This was merely days after she was struck in a head-on collision by another driver who was under the influence. If there was ever a moment for a revengeful heart, and one the world might be fully expecting, losing his wife in that manner would certainly fit the bill. Monty didn't cave and succumb to a corruptive state of hate; he used his pedestal and put his God-given ability to forgive on display for all to see. Monty astounded me with the genuine mercy and grace he extended toward the other family for the loss of their loved one. Is there someone in your life to whom you need to offer forgiveness? Perhaps the burden you have borne for so long now doesn't seem quite as impossible to relinquish.

Joy in the Midst of Suffering

Another bright, illuminating star was a dear friend who confided in Holly and me when her marriage was under attack by Satan. During our conversations, I remember my amazement for the calm she expressed during her storm of infidelity. The couple's vows were publicly declared not even a year beforehand, so this grave concern came as a surprise. Apparently some demons existed in his past, but she was hopeful her husband would remain faithful with the constant reminder of a ring on his finger. Even though he was still purposely and heavily entrenched in sin without any sign of remorse, she didn't seek revenge or call it quits; she reinforced her love and reminded him of their commitment to God and each other. With her gentle ways, she assured him he wasn't the real enemy; she told him he was still beautiful in her eyes, and divorce wasn't an option. When conversing back and forth, I was deeply moved, and even energized, by the combination of her poetic genius and unwavering conviction. I think she could have easily written Psalm 151.

Adding to the sanctity of the situation, my friend's sister (who battles a myriad of chronic health issues) possesses a supernatural ability; the Holy Spirit appears to her in physical manifestation as a thick, dense fog. During an intimate conversation between my friend and her sister in those dark days of despair, her sister actually saw the Holy Spirit flood the room. That is the definition of joy in the midst of suffering. My friend was filled with a deep and abiding peace that only comes from one source. What a wild few months it was, but I am ecstatic to report their relationship has been restored.

Pregnancy Miracles

The last miraculous testament is that of a husband and wife who overcame two taxing pregnancies and deliveries. Our good friends spent sixty nights in the hospital together leading up to the first delivery—she continually cooped up in bed, and he only an arm's length away on a pull-out sofa. It was truly remarkable to watch a mother willingly sacrifice her body for the well-being of her unborn babies. Her husband shared with me that one morning she awoke with tears streaming down her face; she had gained a whole new appreciation for the words in Luke 22:19: "This is my body, which is given for you." After a successful delivery of twins, still seven weeks shy of the due date, they frequented the NICU for another three weeks before coming home as a family of four.

This story would be overwhelming enough if the exhausting eighty-one-day hospital stay was the end; it was not. Their next bundle of joy unexpectedly arrived at twenty-three weeks—an astonishing seventeen weeks before full-term, with only a 10 to 15 percent chance of survival. As a result, many complications arose in the likes of a brain bleed, uncontrolled seizure activity, multiple infections, high-frequency ventilation, heart surgery, and a strong possibility of blindness.

In the midst of this medical chaos, I distinctly remember a conversation he and I shared in the waiting room:

"Do you ever wonder, 'Why me?'" I asked.

"I do," he replied. "But then I realize how it always seems to work out for us, when others haven't been as fortunate. So more importantly I ask, 'Why us?'"

My friend could have easily focused on the obvious storms and referred to their hospital stays as nightmares, but his fortitude from deep within allowed him to focus on the silver lining. As a result, his unwavering trust in God prevailed, and he now enjoys the blessing of three little miracles. To this day, he said they smile when they drive by that hospital, because it reminds them off all the angels on staff who so deeply cared for their babies.

Times of trouble often test a relationship. Generally, a couple's love either buckles under pressure or roots itself even deeper. This power couple has certainly chosen the latter; they continue to strengthen their young, tender marriage even through their challenges. Advertising your faith when the sun is shining isn't any great feat. However, putting its brilliance on display as you helplessly watch your daughter fight for her life, after going through a similar scenario with your firstborn twins, is everything. Their unabashed proclamations, paralleled with those of my friend battling to save her marriage and of Monty preaching during his life-changing tragedy, are ever-contagious. Drawing encouragement from the steadfast faith of others allows us to be strong when our trials inevitably come.

Chapter 21

UNITING THE ROOM:
BELIEVERS AND NONBELIEVERS

$\mathcal{G}$od loves us all the same. Why is it so hard for us to love one another? It's okay for us to disagree, but we should respect our differences instead of using them as motive to viciously attack and go for blood. There is so much animosity and, to be honest, downright hate in our world today. God is love; it must absolutely break His heart to witness the malice we have toward one another. I would be filling oceans with my tears if I had to watch the same horrific scenes that He sees from above each day. The emotional and physical onslaught of bigotry and discrimination seems to be escalating by the minute. I'm not here to debate the heavily heated topics, but I will share my two cents. Judgment isn't the answer; it's not our position to condone or condemn. There is a judge, and I am not He. Here are my ultimate and universal questions to each one of you: Are your motives pure? Do you live with the intention of pleasing God?

Last Call

I believe with all my heart that so many in this day and age desperately lack a dedication to faith. As I've repeatedly stated, this virtue is the gravitational pull that grounds me and centers my conscience, while also leaving me daydreaming of the wonders of entering heaven. I encourage you to live and breathe His word. If you are ridiculed in your discipleship, stand firm, remain loyal to His stewardship, and relish in the refreshing words of 2 Corinthians 2:16-17: "To those who are perishing, we are a dreadful smell of death and doom. But to those who are being saved, we are a life-giving perfume. And who is adequate for such a task as this? You see, we are not like the many hucksters who preach for personal profit. We preach the word of God with sincerity and with Christ's authority, knowing that God is watching us."

As this curtain comes to a close, I greatly thank you for accompanying me on this journey. In my mission of enlightening you with a love for Jesus, I too have assumed the role and gained a renewed perspective. While temporarily exploring a secular stance, I still hold fast to Him as my Rock where I find refuge. I am so humbled by God's continuous mercy and everlasting grace. When I envision meeting our Father in heaven, Mercy Me's "I Can Only Imagine" simultaneously overwhelms my mind and invigorates my soul. Knowing I am only a minuscule, yet special, fraction to complete God's masterpiece is more than I can even fathom.

Visualize the ironic emptiness of a nearly completed two-thousand-piece puzzle with one lonely stowaway still hiding in the box. Each of the pieces is required to occupy a specific space. The other 1,999 simply cannot be substituted for one another, no matter how many times you attempt to turn or force them; even if you *make* them fit, the image of the completed puzzle won't be the same. You share a striking resemblance here on earth. You have been assigned a particular purpose—one that others can't accomplish for you. This is your moment of truth. There has never been a more important time than now for you to do what you are called to do. Find inspiration from Esther 4:14: "Who knows if perhaps you were made queen for just such a time as this?" After hearing these words, she recognized the magnitude of her moment to make a difference. This biblical heroine risked her life and used her God-given courage to save a nation. What about you? You may have your own agenda, but I promise it will never compare to what God has in store for you. Can you hear the urgency of His voice in your ear? Listen. Perhaps you were made *for a time such as this.*

Chapter 22

FROM THE LIVING WORD: NOAH'S CHILDLIKE OBEDIENCE

*F*aith jumps off the manuscript when patrolling the Bible. In fact, a powerful example is unveiled early on, as we are introduced to a pioneer named Noah. As you will quickly discover in your study of scripture, there is a repetitive cycle of a generation that pleases the Lord, followed by the next that is quick to bring disappointment. Noah came into play at a time when he stood alone as a man after God's own heart, while the rest of the human race exploded with wickedness. According to Genesis, he was born to offer comfort.

The previous generation enjoyed lengthy lifespans, often 800 and 900 years long; Methuselah takes the cake at 969. However, with their offspring's desires only concentrated on evil, God became deeply troubled and determined to wipe the face of the earth clean. In that mind-set, our heavenly Father could have easily decided we weren't worth the headache and ended any hopes of you and me ever taking a single breath. In stepped our champion, who found favor in God's eyes and proved there was still goodness on earth. I like to visualize a rescue team scanning the waters for any survivors of a shipwreck. Perhaps in God's deliberation of allowing us a second chance, He too surveyed the souls and was met with frustration and disappointment as He deemed one after another to be corrupt. When

He was all but convinced to permanently rid the world of the human race, there stood Noah: the radiant jewel who couldn't be overlooked. He was the sole illuminating presence enveloped by miles of hate, and God wasn't about to let him flicker out. St. Francis of Assisi paints us a picture with these prophetic words: "All the darkness in the world cannot extinguish the light of a single candle." This powerful symbolism doubles as a reminder that God always wins. Sin can wreak havoc and may triumph in many battles, but God has already claimed victory in the ultimate war.

It's about time we address the elephant in the room if we are going to continue talking about Noah. Why, and specifically how, does one go about building a giant boat? When I say giant, I'm referring to the ark assembled from cypress wood that was nearly 1.5 times the length (450 ft.) and almost half the width (75 ft.) of a football field, while towering over four stories in height (45 ft.). What's even more mind-boggling is the duration of construction, which scholars believe to have ranged from fifty-five to seventy-five years. So the answer to my introductory question would be, under careful guidance and direction from the Divine Contractor.

Remember that the earth was filled with immorality and violence in God's sight. As a result, He was determined to bring floodwaters to destroy all life. Noah and his family were the one exception. God established a covenant with them to repopulate the world, and in turn, be the earthly origin of the bloodline of Christ Jesus. God bestowed upon Noah an auditory blueprint that contained a very detailed set of instructions, precisely down to the type of wood, the specific dimensions, and the passengers that would accompany him two by two (furry, feathered, and four-legged). Genesis 6:22 states: "So Noah did everything exactly as God had commanded him." We forget the importance of that line.

The Bible says our hero was righteous, blameless, and faithful in his walk with God. In essence, he was everything the rest of the world failed to be. He likely wouldn't have been the one to win a popularity contest amongst his peers. Can you relate? Are you often ebbing when everyone else is flowing? Be humbled in the Almighty's current, because there is no alternate force as absolute. And as we shall see, with God's guidance, you can accomplish amazing feats that otherwise seem (and others may deem) unattainable.

Let's draw a parallel between God's holy calling of Noah and today's world. Picture yourself in a crowd with thousands of your fellow men and women, as you eagerly listen to the President of the United States address the country. Just as his speech concludes, he pauses. Before you know it, he has summoned you on stage to present you with a key to the White House. Of all the possible U.S. citizens, you have been selected to fulfill a new position of incredible influence to shape our country's future. *Surprised* probably doesn't even begin to describe it. When you awoke that morning, you had no intention of receiving such a prestigious honor from the president himself. Try to capture that initial reaction and apply it to the incomparable gravity of Noah's mission.

If entering the White House as part of an elect cabinet seems incomprehensible, kick around the idea of possessing the only key to sustaining life. Noah might have very well asked the same question Moses did when leading his people out of Egypt (yet another amazing story in its own right), "Why me?" When your almighty Father comes knocking, it would behoove you to answer the door. While an earthly parent instills confidence in you, a nod from God guarantees you limitless potential.

Hopefully, you are starting to grasp my thesis statement: God has a mission for you. You may feel like you aren't enough or don't have what it takes. You aren't and you don't, but He is and He does. Author Henry T. Blackaby allows us to dream big with this compelling reminder: "God doesn't call the qualified; He qualifies the called." Look no further than the patriarchs of the Bible for great examples; pay special attention to the before-and-after stories surrounding their encounters with God. Reading from Matthew 14:22–33, I am trying to learn from Saint Peter's mistakes. When I concentrate on my own fear in the storm, I sink; when I keep my eyes fixed on Jesus, I can walk on water. And when you have a level of faith that allows you to walk on water, you can move mountains. The first mention of moving mountains may sound impossible. Rather than concentrating on the ultimate goal, be obedient to His call—no matter how small. After all, Noah didn't begin his journey of faith building a crazy-huge boat; he worked up to it by obeying God in the daily mundane. What ARK (act of random kindness) is He asking you to undertake today? Your response to the call of duty in God's army may be the missing puzzle piece for someone else's salvation. Let's make Christ proud as we await His return.

Part 5

MOVING FORWARD

Forward: *Of, relating to, or done in preparation for the future.*
—The American Heritage College Dictionary

Great is his faithfulness; his mercies begin afresh each morning.
—Lamentations 3:23

Chapter 23

YOUR NEW LIFE AWAITS

Whether it's role models and influences, relationships, vocations, or faith, they are all critical and harness the potential to operate in a synergistic fashion to add value to your life. Throughout the course of this ride, I have thrown a lot your way to ponder. It can be very frustrating when someone encourages you to make a change in your life, yet leaves you with a vague message without any concrete ideas of how to take that first step. Thus, I will lay some specific recommendations at your feet, in an attempt to provide you with solid footing for the road ahead.

Don't dwell on the yesterdays, letting a negative past affect your opportunity for success. Be honest with yourself; you may not be living the life you intended. There may be mishaps or misfortune in your rearview mirror; leave them there. The good (rather, the great) news is that these words found in Lamentations 3:23 are true: "His mercies begin afresh each morning." Every day you wake up is a new day. Spend the rest of today reflecting on your current situation and deciding what areas of your life need improvement. Formulate a list of long-term goals for where you see yourself in one, five, and ten years. Then, as equally important, add short-term goals to help keep you on track. Post these goals where they will be visible on a daily basis (by your bed, above the bathroom sink, on the refrigerator, next to the front door, etc.) so that drive to attain them becomes engrained in you. Let tomorrow be day one toward achieving a brighter future.

Where to Start

- Enter into a relationship with your Creator. What better way to understand life than to accept His offer. Fall to your knees, bow your head, and say a simple prayer inviting Jesus Christ into your life. Ask Him to come inside your heart, guide you on a daily basis, and show you the right way to live. Admittedly so, the Bible can be very daunting at first glance; still to this day, it remains overwhelming to me at times. However, when you are able to favorably navigate the word and learn from His teachings, you will appreciate this treasure for what it is: invaluable knowledge containing answers for all of life's problems. In addition to studying scripture, Matthew Kelly's Prayer Process can provide a twenty-four-hour reflection and daily guide to help you develop a more intimate relationship with God. (It has been life-changing for me.)

- Send cards to five to ten people who have made a significant impact on you. In a world of social media, electronic transcription can suffice; I would also argue that nothing is better than an unexpected handwritten letter or a personal visit. In the days ahead, surround yourself with those who build you up and drive you to be the best version of yourself.

- Begin to realize the world is bigger than you and your needs. Temporarily step outside your four walls and volunteer for a day. A homeless shelter, soup kitchen, humane society, or other local charity might be a good first option. Simply start, and if it goes well, aim for quarterly or even monthly commitments. You don't have to go crazy, overwhelm yourself, and be committed every day of the week. Even once a month may sound like you are giving up a lot of your freedom, but we are only talking about a dozen days out of a calendar year. Seems easy when you think of it like that, huh? Then, watch how those twelve days (or whatever you decide) give you a fresh perspective and completely change your mind-set the other 353 days. Trust me.

- Live each day by the Golden Rule; it's no mistake you have heard this before. Remember the book of James in the moments frustration sets in: "Be quick to listen, slow to speak, and slow to get angry." Recognize that no one can force a reaction upon you. Don't give your enemies so much power. Others may be strong instigators and push you to the edge, but the response elicited is ultimately up to you and you alone. Hate and resentment are heavy burdens to bear. Sure, you are human, and there will be days when you emotionally break, but strive for those to be few and far between. You hold the key to your own happiness.

- Count your blessings, right where you are. Likely, you have everything you need but not necessarily want. Understand that essential difference.

- Make health a priority with proper nutrition and exercise. Dr. Ann Kulze's *Eat Right for Life* book series is a fantastic resource to propel you into transforming the contents inside your fridge, freezer, and pantry. If you currently dine out every night, try implementing a schedule to cook at home once a week. Keep building on your progress and work steadily to turn the tide. As far as being active, find a type of exercise you enjoy (or even tolerate). Start low and go slow. If this is your first rodeo, be patient. You will likely not love those first couple of weeks. Your body will be tired, sore, hot, and adamantly screaming for you to throw in the towel. Entertain mixing up different activities, duration, and intensity levels. Encourage others to join you for added accountability. Before you know it, your newfound hobby will become part of your routine, and you will leave your previously sedentary lifestyle in the dust. After all, we are instructed to take care of our temple.

Rapid-Fire Last-Minute Pep Talk

Avoid simply going through the motions, day in and day out. Life is far too short and delicate to let it waste away. Escape the urge to fall in line with the crowd. Be the exception. Find joy in what others pass off as mundane. Give 110 percent to every task required of you, no matter the level of importance. Seize each moment of opportunity. Make a meaningful difference in the world. Live with passion and purpose. Love unconditionally. Confidently hold your head high, offer a smile to the multitude, and when asked for the source of your happiness, be a witness to our Maker's greatness.

In repeating my plea from the introduction, remember: Perspective is the key that unlocks true happiness. Each day you wake up, try to replace the questions of "What do I want for myself?" and "How can I make myself happy?" with "What does He want for me?" and "How can I make Him happy?"

Follow Mary's lead in John 12:3 and give your best to God. For her, it was an alabaster jar of expensive perfume that she poured over the feet of Jesus. And let us never forget: God gave us His best when He sacrificed His Son. Now, it's time for us to bring Paul's words from Romans 12:1-2 to life:

> "And so, dear brothers and sisters, I plead with you to give your bodies to God because of all he has done for you. Let them be a living and holy sacrifice—the kind he will find acceptable. This is truly the way to worship him. Don't copy the behavior and customs of this world, but let God transform you into a new person by changing the way you think. Then you will learn to know God's will for you, which is good and pleasing and perfect."

With that selfless and newly discovered conviction, break open your box for God. Let His creativity piece together the rest of your life and and allow Him to use you as His instrument to deeply enrich the lives of others. Please share this book and spread His message. May God abundantly bless you!

REFERENCES

The American Heritage College Dictionary. 4th ed. (Boston: Houghton Mifflin Company, 2002), 500, 546, 1173, 1204, 1535.

Broocks, Rice. *Man, Myth, Messiah: Answering History's Greatest Question.* Nashville: W Publishing Group, 2016.

Chapman, Gary. *The 5 Love Languages: The Secret to Love that Lasts.* Chicago: Northfield, 2010, Kindle edition.

"For King & Country—'It's Not Over Yet': The Story Behind the Song". https://www.youtube.com/watch?v=xaSM1G37yhU. Published on July 17, 2014.

God's Not Dead. DVD. Pure Flix Productions, 2014.

Hamilton, Adam. *Making Sense of the Bible: Rediscovering the Power of Scripture Today.* New York: HarperCollins, 2014.

Kelly, Matthew. *The Prayer Process.* http://dynamiccatholic.com/four-signs-of-a-dynamic-catholic/prayer-process/

Kelly, Matthew. *What If It Were Your Only Son?* 100PercentCatholic. com. https://www.youtube.com/watch?v=KofgSBmweJA. Published on June 21, 2010.

Kendrick, Stephen, Alex Kendrick, and Randy Alcorn. *The Resolution for Men.* Nashvilile: B&H Publishing Group, 2011.

Kulze, Dr. Ann G. *Eat Right for Life: Your Common Sense Guide to Eating Right and Living Well*. Omaha: WELCOA, 2011.

McLeod, S. A. (2016). Maslow's Hierarchy of Needs. Retrieved from www.simplypsychology.org/maslow.html

The Paradoxical Commandments are reprinted with the permission of the author. (c) Copyright Kent M. Keith 1968, renewed 2001, www.paradoxicalcommandments.com.

Scripture quotations are taken from the Holy Bible, New Living Translation, copyright © 1996, 2004, 2007 by Tyndale House Foundation. Used by permission of Tyndale House Publishers, Inc., Carol Stream, Illinois. All rights reserved.

Strobel, Lee. *The Case for Christ: A Journalist's Personal Investigation of the Evidence for Jesus*. Grand Rapids: Zondervan, 2016.

"Tenth Avenue North Part 2: Story Behind 'Worn'". Wally Show. https://www.youtube.com/watch?v=P2niY4LlbJk. Published on July 12, 2013

Wallace, J. Warner. *Cold-Case Christianity: A Homicide Detective Investigates the Claims of the Gospels*. Colorado Springs: David C Cook, 2013.

Young, Wm. Paul. *The Shack: Where Tragedy Confronts Eternity*. Newbury Park: Windblown Media, 2007.

ABOUT THE AUTHOR

 att Plank was born and raised in Pittsburg, KS. He graduated from Pittsburg State University with a Bachelor of Arts in Psychology and from the University of Kansas with a Doctorate in Pharmacy. Practicing as a pharmacist, he enjoys his opportunity to help improve the health of those in the community, coach his patients to a healthier lifestyle, and inspire others to be their best, while spreading his love for Christ to any and all. Matt currently resides in Andover, KS with his wife, Holly, and their two young children.

CPSIA information can be obtained
at www.ICGtesting.com
Printed in the USA
FSHW021354010419
56812FS